2/11/80

Family Matters

Family
Matters

BY LAWRENCE H. FUCHS

 RANDOM HOUSE, NEW YORK

First Printing
Copyright © 1972 by Lawrence H. Fuchs
All rights reserved under International and Pan-American Copyright
Conventions. Published in the United States by Random House, Inc.,
New York, and simultaneously in Canada by Random House of
Canada Limited, Toronto.

Library of Congress Cataloging in Publication Data
Fuchs, Lawrence H
Family matters.
Bibliography: p.
1. Family—United States.   2. United States—
Social conditions—1960–   I. Title.
HQ536.F9   301.42'0973   78-37037
ISBN 0-394-47548-8

Manufactured in the United States of America

To Betty, and to life

Preface

Six years ago I began to teach a seminar on the family at Brandeis University. The more I studied the history of American families compared with that of families elsewhere, the more I became convinced that there were unusual pressures on Americans which caused conflict within families and separated members of families from each other. I began to realize that the conflict between generations and between sexes resulted in large measure from a family system in the United States which stressed independence and equality in personal relationships to a degree unknown elsewhere in history.

During the past six years many angry books have been written on family relationships. Apparently we live in an age of angry feelings blatantly expressed and acted on. Radical women and the militant young have often adopted the rhetoric of spokesmen for angry Black Americans. American society, they assert, oppresses them.

But the history of white women and the young has been vastly different from the history of the subjugation of Blacks. From the seventeenth century on in America, both the young and women acquired more freedom, power and status than did the women and children of any other major civilization in history. That fact may provide little or no comfort to angry women or to the young. They know what they feel and what they want. And much of what they ask seems right to me.

Yet, even deeply held feelings cannot be trusted as the only basis for wise living. The more I read or heard about conflict in families, the more it seemed to me that all of us—husbands, wives, children, grandparents, parents—needed to root our feelings in a better understanding of the history of American families. Soon I began to see that it was not enough to understand the history of American families. In addition to a historical perspective, it was important to ask why and how American families were different from those in other societies. Then I began to realize, too, that an evolutionary and biological perspective was needed before one could understand what it means to be a human infant or child, a human parent or spouse. It was necessary to ask not just what is American about American families but what is human about human families.

I hope I have asked the right questions and that the answers will help readers gain a better understanding of their own family situations.

April 20, 1972   Lawrence H. Fuchs

Acknowledgments

First, to those Brandeis students who, for the past six years in my course on the family, have looked with me into the question of the distinctiveness of American families. They have written dozens of superb original papers comparing aspects of the American family with those of families in other cultures, drawing on biography and autobiography, family records, poetry, short stories, novels, musical theater, serious drama, cartoons, popular music, comic strips, newspapers, magazines, films, photographs, and children's literature and games. Also, they have taught me much about their own generation and family life through personal documentaries and rich, sensitive conversations.

I have been particularly lucky in having two research assistants during the past three years whose help has been invaluable: Roberta Pressman, who made a brilliant record at Brandeis more than ten years ago and who is now a wonderful teacher, wife and mother; and Marilyn Halter, who graduated from Brandeis in 1971 after writing a superb honors thesis on the relationship of Protestant revivalism in the nineteenth century to basic-encounter groups in the twentieth. Both of these women know their way around books and ideas. They were more than assistants; they were excellent critics. Reading the manuscripts at various stages and generous in their help were three friends, Clare Wofford, Lila Ballendorf, Janet Hanley, and my brother, Victor Fuchs, who has always been a tough and constructive critic.

I have been blessed with secretaries who do more than type, file and keep the schedule. Grace Short at Brandeis has been patient and warm-hearted in putting up with the relentless pressure of deadlines despite her many other activities. Sandra Stevens is much more than a skillful secretary. A wise friend, counselor and critic, she contributed much to this book's development. My debt to her is large.

To Steve Whitfield, my colleague at Brandeis, thanks for suggesting the title. To Gerard McCauley, much appreciation for encouragement, advice and helpful suggestions. To Robert Loomis, editor and friend, whose patient, sharp questions helped me to clarify my thinking and to reword key paragraphs in every chapter, I am particularly grateful. To Sono Rosenberg, gratitude for helpful copy-editing.

Finally, three members of my family gave me special help. My daughter Frances read Chapters II and III, and my daughter Naomi read Chapter II. Both made suggestions which I adopted. My wife, Betty, a skillful editor in her own right, carefully read the manuscript at each phase and made many significant editorial contributions. But most important, she gave loving encouragement and enthusiasm to the project from beginning to end.

Deficiencies, of which there are many, were not always caught by my family, friends or colleagues, and they are, of course, my responsibility.

Contents

tion for Personal Achievement · The Great American
Discipline Debate · Achieve, Achieve! (and Enjoy?)
· On Being an American Adolescent · Adolescent
Loneliness · Awareness-Overload · Choice-Overload ·
Schools Are Part of the Problem · Rejecting the Effi-
ciency Ethic · Expression as Experience · Groping for
New Values · The Authentic Self? · Fleeing from and
Fighting Depression · Dependency Is a Dirty Word
for the Young and the Old

III ON BEING FEMALE IN AMERICA   90

The Rationalization of Male Dominance · The Re-
discovery of Eve · The Double Standard under Attack
· The Sexual Revolution Has an Early Beginning ·
"Meddling in Such Things as Are Proper for Men"
· Toward Equal Rights through Law · A New View
of Divorce · Power at Home · Super Mother in
America · American Husbands and Motherolotry ·
Patriarchy, No; Competition, Yes! · What Do They
Want? · Women and Their Bodies · Women and
Their Minds · Equality: Biology and Culture · The
Differences That Biological Differences Make · The
Rejection of Motherhood

IV FLIGHT FROM FAMILIES   150

The Price of Individualism · Fleeing from Families ·
The Joiners · The Saving Cause · The New Religion:
Self-Discovery and Love through Psychotherapy ·
Basic Encounter Groups: Families Away from Fami-
lies · Making Contact: The Personals · New Forms of
Families: The Commune Movement · Strengthen-
ing the Family through Sexual Freedom? · Reinvent-
ing the Nuclear Family

Family Matters

I The American-ness of It All

The nuclear family—mother, father and children—is in a time of transition and strain. Many of its critics, particularly among the young and women, see the family as the primary enemy of human individuality. The attacks on the family by psychologists such as David Cooper in his book *The Death of the Family* and by dozens of less popular writers are reminiscent of the diagnosis and predictions made by psychologist John B. Watson, the founder of the behaviorist school of psychology, more than forty years ago. Watson and many of his followers predicted then that marriage and the family as Americans knew it would be dead in fifty years. At this writing there are nearly ten years to go. The family, although in serious trouble, is still with us. The attacks continue, but the family remains the most universal of human institutions.

Since human beings are capable of destroying, creating and adapting, predictions as to the long-term future of the human family are risky. The family evolved as a product of human culture; no matter how powerful the forces which created it, it is possible that one day it will be dissolved or at least radically altered. In any case, Americans particularly are feeling the tension of family life. The question is: Why?

There is no way to answer that question effectively without trying to understand something of the evolution of human families and the American-ness of families in the United States.

Despite an evolutionary history which emphasizes dependence as the most human feature of human families, Americans have pursued independence as an ideal in family relationships. In America, children are taught and learn to fear dependence. Wary husbands guard their independence; angry women now proclaim it. Many American women, now more than ever, demand independence and equality without taking into account the fact that differences in many sex roles and functions stem in large measure from the evolution of human families. Thus, the essential source of tension for members of American families has been the conflict between their commitment to the ideals of independence and equality and the conditions of dependency and inequality which mark human families and societies.

Consider the contemporary young mother who feels imprisoned by her hyperactive, demanding son; the adolescent who feels that his parents, having urged him in childhood to be experimental, do not let him do what he wants to do; or the middle-aged wife who suddenly realizes that she has been in many ways what no one in the United States should ever be—a servant. Think of the older sister who measures every favor and privilege given to her younger brother to make certain that she does not lose out. Or the father and husband who worries and wonders why his requests (orders?) are barely listened to, let alone respected. Or the aging grandparents saddened by children or grandchildren who struggle and blunder through the tortuous process of growing up but who do not seek advice from their elders. While such feelings would be extraordinary in most of the world, they are commonplace in the United States. Far from being idiosyncratic, they derive from a family system with deep roots in the American experience. It is not an industrial or urban or twentieth-century system, since it existed in large measure for Americans—in contrast to others—when they were still overwhelmingly an agricultural people. It is a system which turns upside down five to six thousand years of social history in the Western world and which challenges the evolutionary bases of human families as we know them.

THE EVOLUTION OF HUMAN FAMILIES

What is most universal about human families—a long helpless, mother-dependent childhood, long-term sexual pairing between adult males and females and considerable postnatal fathering—has a history which is now possible to reconstruct from fossil evidence accumulating at an extremely rapid rate (more fossils were collected in 1970 than in all previous years put together).

It was probably three to four million years ago that the predecessors of our own species, *Homo sapiens*, first stood upright on two legs on the grassy plains of Africa and began to use their hands in order to make tools to protect themselves and to hunt animals for meat.* A great movement of glaciers had denuded the forests and exposed the ancestors of humans to dangers from larger, swifter, stronger animals on the plains; these meat-eating hominids (the human species and its ancestors) depended more and more on their skill as makers of weapons and other tools and on communication and cooperation among themselves to survive.

In becoming more human, hominids trusted their instincts less and what they could learn and teach more. Creating language and learning how to store knowledge and pass it on from generation to generation, they developed larger brains capable of housing an increasingly intricate network of electrical circuits. With the doubling of brain size between three or four and one million years

---

* Chimpanzees, who are primates like humans and more like them than the other apes (gorillas, gibbons or orangutans), have been seen to kill and eat a monkey, but that is rare; they and other primates remained essentially vegetarian.

ago, hominid heads grew much larger in proportion to the rest of their bodies compared with other primates. The brain eventually grew so large in relation to the rest of the body (a ratio of 1 to 30 for humans compared with 1 to 230 for gorillas) that nature was faced with a difficult reproductive problem. At birth the infant's brain had to be big enough to begin the learning process, but could not be so large as to endanger a mother's life in pregnancy or during birth. Two factors had to be balanced: the health and mobility of the mother and the relative helplessness of the infant. A compromise was effected. Human infants are born with brains one-third the size they will become by maturity, compared with three-fourths for chimpanzees (our closest relatives), but large enough to make them unusually efficient learners.

To accommodate the growth of larger heads for a longer time in utero, the hominid female's pelvis was widened considerably in relation to the rest of her body (reducing her mobility more than that of other primate females), and pregnancy was extended to nine months, compared with seven for the chimp (the ape most like us) or the six for the baboon (the monkey that lives on the ground much of the time). If nature had widened female hips further, allowing for a longer fetal period, mothers would have been immobilized even more, possibly endangering their survival. The essence of the compromise was that hominid infants, of all the primates, were born needing a much longer time to learn how to take care of themselves, but with a much greater capacity for learning how to cooperate in order to do so. Compared with other primates, they are helpless. They can cling, but not enough to support their own weight. They cannot lift their head at birth; and they have the least well-developed nervous system.

For the mother, this means giving close, careful attention to infants far longer after birth than do other primate mothers. Monkey infants learn to walk within a month, nonhuman apes within six, while humans often take as long as eighteen months or more. Male chimpanzees wander off from their mothers for days at a time at age four or five; and by seven or eight, female chimps are ready to mate.

Because hominid females stood on their hind legs, they developed large, protruding breasts, an anatomical feature unknown to other animals. They provided a warm, soft, pleasurable bed for helpless infants, who, in turn, rewarded their mothers with tingling sensuous feelings when they were held to the breast and suckled for milk. This remarkable anatomical change in hominid females was accompanied by two other unusual biological developments which also helped infants and children to survive. The first was menopause, the elimination of the menstrual cycle in females in their late forties, allowing human females to complete their responsibilities as mothers until their youngest reached maturity. In addition, estrus (often called "heat"), an uncontrollable physiological state of sexual desire and receptivity, was eliminated in the human female. The females of all other mammals give themselves to short periods of intense, almost maniacal sexual activity during estrus in which their offspring have to fend for themselves, a situation which would doom human infants.*

Exactly when the other two distinctive characteristics of human families—long-term sexual pairing and the invention of cultural fatherhood—developed no one knows, but it certainly occurred while our ancestors were leading what the anthropologists call a hunter-gatherer existence. Males hunted for meat; females remained at home base, gathered vegetables, and cared for their offspring. With the end of estrus came the possibility of choice in the timing of sexual relations. Females, like males, might desire and be receptive to sex at any time. By developing an attachment to individual females with whom it was possible to have sexual relations at any time after returning from the hunt rather than just in their estrus period, males developed long-term relationships with their mates and offspring. In addition, the development of large breasts probably promoted front-to-front sex—unknown to other primates—further personalizing the sex act. It was undoubtedly common for many mothers to mate with the same father; at other times many males mated with one mother; sometimes there may have been a series of pair bonds or perhaps even lifelong pairing between one male and one female. With the invention of fire, at least 750,000 years ago, male hunters drove other animals from caves, and with females and children warm and safe from predators, males were

---

* Other primate mothers do not experience estrus in the last phase of pregnancy and the earliest postnatal phase. Chimp females are usually in estrus for six to ten days out of a thirty-five-day cycle.

able to roam farther in search of big game. If they returned without meat, there would be hardship for all, but at least the females might have gathered enough vegetables and roots to keep them alive. If males returned with meat, they would share it with females and children. By feeding children they became fathers even before they recognized their features in their own offspring or understood the biology of fatherhood. Those males who were skillful in feeding and protecting their females and children and those females who nurtured their children well would have had reason to be thankful and loving toward each other.*

FATHERHOOD AND PATRIARCHY

In no other one of the two billion animal species that have existed has there been anything comparable to the long-term investment of energy which human males have made in postnatal fathering In only about 5 percent of the animal species have males shown any interest in their offspring, but almost all birds help raise the young to some extent for short periods of time. Male as well as female pigeons surprisingly produce milk with which they feed their young; but the young pigeon is soon able to fly and no longer needs a father. Phalarope males sit on four large female-produced eggs for about twenty days until the eggs hatch and then protect the young for a

---

* Chimps do not pair up at all. They are totally promiscuous. The gibbon, another ape, comes closest to humans in this respect. Among them a single female and male live for some time together with their young, and each drives off others of the same sex. Among the monkeys, baboons mate for a few days and separate.

short while until they can fend for themselves. But these are peculiar cases and among the mammals fatherly care is exceptional. Wolves and foxes bring food to nursing mothers and infants, and many male monkeys defend females and the young from hostile outsiders, but they do not even seem to know their own children. Fatherhood is a human specialty.

Ever since the 1890's, anthropologists and philosophers have speculated on the origins of patriarchy. By "patriarchy" I mean not just the governance of society by adult males but specifically the governance of households of one or more families. Before fathers attached themselves to particular females and children in a continuing relationship, and before kinship relationships were recognized, mothers undoubtedly had the responsibility for setting and enforcing limits for their small children as well as for nurturing them. There are many mother-child-household societies today where fathers do not live at home. But even these are patriarchal, whether they are ruled by the father or by the mother's male relatives. Despite commonly held assumptions and ingenious speculations to the contrary, there has probably never been a matriarchal society or family system. They may have existed; they may exist at some future time, but no competent ethnographer or historian has uncovered one.

One reason for the confusion is that in many societies the residence of a family (father, mother and children) belongs to the mother or her relatives—matrilocal—and/or the descent of children is counted in the line of the mother's family—matrilineal—but even in those rare societies where adult females hold formal authority in families, actual rule is in the hands of their male relatives. Magnificent and commanding female leaders of tribes and kingdoms have appeared throughout the ages, but there have been no known matriarchies, if by that term is meant a society in which families generally are ruled in fact, not just in form, by adult females.

With the invention of fatherhood in hunter-gatherer societies, patriarchy may not have been inevitable—and it certainly is not inevitable today—but the specialization of functions between adult males and females probably encouraged it.* Males on the hunt tended to become mesomorphic (muscular and big-boned), and they became specialists in the use of weapons. Females tended toward endomorphism (fat, round body structure) because of their relatively sedentary life. Sheer physical strength and skill in weaponry probably meant that males assumed authority to command as well as to protect families and clans from hostile outsiders and internal divisions.

As clans became larger and more complex, internal conflict must have been a constant threat. Only adult males were strong enough to control their growing sons should they threaten their mothers, sisters or other members of the clan. It is difficult to imagine how stability

* Although there is an account of one society of hunter-gatherers, the Mbute Pygmies of the Congo, in which decisions are made entirely by group (a band of about thirty families) without, it is alleged, authority being held by anyone—neither by adult males nor by females —the account does not accord with what is known to be the case in other hunter-gatherer societies that have been studied extensively by competent ethnographers. They are all patriarchies.

within families and clans could have been achieved without patriarchy. Before the invention of fatherhood and partiarchy, it seems almost certain that males dominated females without much consideration for them or their offspring. In this sense, patriarchy became the basis of civilization itself. By bringing relative stability to family life, patriarchy made possible the accumulation of knowledge over time without which *Homo sapiens* could not possibly have survived. Through children whom they claimed as their own, hominid males glimpsed the future and the importance of preparing their offspring for it. With affection for women and children toward whom they felt some responsibility, there was incentive to till the soil as well as to hunt, and to create literature as well as language, technology for comfort as well as war, and rules for "right" conduct as well as for survival. Without patriarchy, it is possible that complex civilizations would not have emerged in the past several thousand years. Neither complex technology nor social organization, art, music or great religious and ethical systems—all based on the accumulation of learned behavior from generation to generation—would have developed without the stable family life which fatherhood and patriarchy made possible.

THE AMERICAN WAY OF FAMILIES

The evolution of human families took hundreds of thousands of years, the development of an American family system less than one hundred. The forces which gave birth to the American family system were strikingly different in combination from those which appeared elsewhere: dissident Protestants who founded the nation stressed personal faith through a direct encounter with God as the road to salvation, an emphasis which ultimately encouraged individualism for all against patriarchal rule; immigrants to the New World were already somewhat independent of the patriarchal families they left behind, and in America they found a relative abundance of land and resources where labor and women were in short supply, making both women and children more valuable than they had ever been in the old country. As a result, women and children sought and achieved a degree of independence from patriarchal authority which they never had before. Experiencing some, they wanted more. Thus began a family system noted for its dispersive, competitive characteristics. When seen from a cross-cultural point of view—Latin-Catholic, Hindu, Chinese, Moslem, East European, or even North European—the early and continuing emphasis on personal independence and equality stands out.

Thomas Jefferson's claim in his first draft of the Declaration of Independence "that all men are created equal and *independent*" (italics are mine) offered a prescription for American life based on an obvious myth about *Homo sapiens*. Tapeworms are equal. Human beings are unequal in experience, ability, judgment and responsibility. Eels and salmon, born without parents, are independent. Clearly, humans are not.

Of course, Jefferson was making a political point. He meant that human beings should be treated on a basis of equal justice because of their essential humanity and that they should be freed from the shackles of arbitrary, authoritarian controls. Although Jefferson's point about independence and equality was political, Americans began to apply it to family relationships despite the fact of human dependency and inequality. By "independence," they have usually meant the right to make choices without being bound by someone else's authority; by "equality," the right to receive benefits and privileges similar to those held by others in the family.

THE SACRED COW OF INDEPENDENCE

Independence has been seen as the greatest good, even justifying discriminatory treatment against those who do not espouse and practice it. In part, the Roman Catholic Church has been seen as challenging the American ideal. To some extent, immigrants from Asia and eastern and southern Europe have been viewed similarly. Many Americans have been able to rationalize their treatment of American Indians and foreigners precisely because these groups have been perceived as nonbelievers in the American ideal of independence.

The ideal of independence has been celebrated in prose, poetry, language, drama, music, art and philosophy in the United States. Review the panoply of outstanding Americans in any field from the American Revolution on, and it will become clear how personal independence is the closest Americans have ever come to forming a national cult. Their civic heroes—from Benjamin Franklin to John F. Kennedy—exemplify it. Their poets—

Emerson, Longfellow, Whittier, Lowell, Dickinson, Robinson, Frost and others—sing about it. Their literature deals insistently with the theme of man against society and/or nature. Take your choice: James Fenimore Cooper's Natty Bumppo or Mark Twain's independent boys who are up and doing; Hawthorne, Melville, Hemingway, Faulkner and the novelists today who write about the lonely, agonizing struggle to assert individuality against society.

Who have been the American folk heroes? The independent pioneer always on the move, performing feats of daring; the lonesome cowboy, altogether unencumbered with family ties; the Horatio Algers who rise by their own bootstraps to great business success; and the gargantuan mythic heroes, such as Paul Bunyan and John Henry, who are ready for action and to make decisions from the moment they are born. Perhaps the greatest of all American folk heroes, John Henry, burst into the world without any need of his parents at all. On his first day, after ordering his mother and father to get him four ham bones, a potful of cabbage, corn bread, pot liquor, biscuits and a big jug full of cane molasses, he walked out of the house and away from them and Black River country forever.

The prophets of American values—from Jefferson to Ralph Waldo Emerson and Henry David Thoreau to William James and John Dewey—have insisted that the individual should trust no one but himself. The ideal man is one who is ready to confront the challenges of life depending only on his unique abilities. He lives and achieves apart from his historical and cultural inheritance. Emerson, whose influence on American education, philosophy and psychology has probably been larger than that of any other American, never tired of urging the individual, "trust thyself . . . nothing is at last sacred but the integrity of your own mind; . . . the only right is what is after my constitution; the wrong is against it." He never asked how man learned to trust himself (if not through being trusted and loved by others) or how he developed his own voice or manner without trustworthy, loving models to follow. For Emerson, not only is every man unique (a banality on which all could agree), but presumably he is sprung full-blown from the head of Zeus and, like John Henry, ready to manage for himself.

Emerson, of course, was reacting to the powerful Puritan controls of his own parents and to an American environment which encouraged an attack on authority and history when he asked, "Cannot we let people be themselves, and enjoy life in their own way? You are trying to make another man *you.* One is enough." Here was the cult of independence stated as strongly as it had ever been before. "No law can be sacred to me but that of my own nature," said Emerson. The sins of Christian morality were expunged from his theology. "Sin," wrote Emerson, "is when a man trifles with himself and is untrue to his own constitution." Perhaps more than any other American, Emerson helped to usher in a new Puritanism, an overwhelming insistence on emotional self-sufficiency, which few were capable of bearing without intense loneliness and anxiety.

The widespread belief in the absolute value of independence has promoted a fear of continuing entanglements with others, particularly a fear of families. Not many have followed Emerson's exhortation, "Let us feel if we will the absolute insulation of men . . . let us even bid our dearest friends farewell, and defy them, saying 'who are you? Unhand me: I will be dependent no more,' " but millions have envied and honored the ideal of being free from prescriptive obligations of any kind, even to friends, but particularly to parents and spouses.

While Americans have generally accepted the ideal of personal independence as an unqualified good, that has not been true of foreign observers. Many of them have seen the effects of the cult of independence as inimical to happiness. Alexis de Tocqueville, the most perceptive of all visitors to America, pointing out that Americans "owe nothing to any man" and "expect nothing from any man" and have acquired the "habit of always considering themselves as standing alone . . ." and as "apt to imagine that their whole destiny is in their hands," concluded in doleful but perhaps not exaggerated terms: "Thus not only does democracy make every man forget his ancestors, but it hides his descendants and separates his contemporaries from him; it throws him back forever upon himself alone and threatens in the end to confine him entirely within the solitude of his own heart." He explained, "The same quality that rends him [the American] independent of each of his fellow citizens, taken separately, exposes him alone and unprotected."

Although the assertion of the independent self has been

the common response of Americans to man's search for identity, most people of the world answer the question "Who are you?" by saying, "I am of Y family and village X." For them the individual grows up through an unending series of dependency relationships within a family. Recognition is given to the unequal capacities and responsibilities of small children, youths and adults. What most Americans would see as unwanted dependency feelings are viewed favorably. In India, for example, where there is no word for dependency, the terms *bandha, sambandha* and *bandhavy* (bond, bondship and kinship) are positive. There and in much of the world the ideal of human maturity is not independence from and within relationships but the maintenance of satisfying, pleasurable and continuous binding relationships. In the United States, by contrast, there evolved the first culture in human history where an increasing number of people drew little psychological strength from roles or relationships, from being able to say, "I am a woman," "I am a mother," "I am a man," "I am a father," "I am the son of L," "My grandfather is of the house of Y," "My ancestors were teachers," and so on.

THE AMERICAN FAMILY AS A SYSTEM

20. 1

The family not only exemplifies the dominant values of the culture but it carries and impresses them on the young. There is the dilemma. With its emphasis on personal independence and equality, American ideology is at war with the very nature of family life, at least as it has been known through the ages. For thousands of years men, women and children in families understood to the depths of their beings how totally dependent they were on each other. When resources were scarce and the family had to be defended against hostile outsiders, the young and the women always needed protection by dominant males, who usually were given positions of command. Biologically, it made sense. Only women became pregnant, suckled and warmed the young. Males were physically stronger. Roles and functions were assigned along hierarchical lines by age and sex. In America a new kind of family system emerged, based on the search of individual members for personal independence.

How to describe such a system? The clearest way is by listing its distinctive characteristics, of which ten are the most important.

The Rejection of the Family of Orientation

The first aspect of the American system is the rejection of the family of orientation, the family from which one has come—one's own parents and grandparents. Only in America was so much emphasis given to separating oneself from one's forbears. In nearly all traditional cultures, and that still means 90 percent of the world's people, the family is idealized or at least obeyed. In traditional families the individual remembers his ancestors, grandparents, godparents, aunts, uncles and cousins. He feels loyalty and obligation to them. In the United States many factors worked against the continuation of traditional families. Frequently immigrants left their grandparents or even their parents behind. Even if they did not, conditions in America were vastly different from those in Europe or Asia. In the old country one's family lived for generations in the same village; here physical mobility put considerable distance between two generations. There the shoemaker's son was likely to become a shoemaker; here occupational mobility meant the opening of new perceptions, attitudes and statuses for each new generation. There grandparents could help in the raising of children; here mothers were much more on their own. Why look back? To bend to the will of one's parents is to bend to the past. Even to accept guidance might compromise one's independence.

The Idealization of the Family of Procreation

One of the bulwarks of the extended family had been the control by parents or grandparents—the elders—over the choice of mates for children. In America that control disappeared quickly. Each new generation insisted on free mate choice, which, reinforced by American optimism and faith in the future, led to a new emphasis on romantic love as the basis for each new nuclear family (husband, wife and children), the family of procreation, which each mother and father begins at marriage. The idealization of the family of procreation is endlessly depicted in prints by Currier and Ives, portraits by Norman Rockwell on the cover of the *Saturday Evening Post*, popular songs ("Just Molly and me and baby makes three in my blue heaven"), the fiction of popular magazines and novels, romantic musical comedy and Hollywood movies.

Having seen the faults of their parents' marriage, the

new couple (often destined to repeat them) intends to do things differently. Each spouse usually brings to marriage a determination to be a good companion, friend and lover, as well as parent and economic helpmate. In many cultures it would be unthinkable that the wife should be a friend. Where but in the United States would a husband try to make his wife into a mistress? Here two partners, freely choosing each other, treat love in marriage rather than marriage itself as a sacrament. It is love that brought them together, a love based on moonlight walks, hushed and intimate conversations and sexual excitement. Having chosen each other for love, they have high hopes for love everlasting. In addition, they have the responsibility for molding (not controlling, heavens no!) a new generation of young without being bound by the dead hand of the past.

The Precocity and Aggressiveness of Small Children

Because, in their ideal family, Americans praised the new and celebrated change, children were welcomed not because of the credit they might bring to the family name but because they were heralds of the future. Parents believed in independence, and they trained their children for self-sufficiency. As a consequence, the third aspect of the American family system, the precocity and aggressiveness of small children, emerged. Even today there is probably no feature of American life which so upsets Western Europeans (perhaps Englishmen most of all) as much as what they see as the self-centeredness of American children. The pressure to make them that way, mainly through performance, begins in the cradle. Grunts, finger wiggles and then first steps are counted and celebrated. Each child is told how precious and different he or she is. Each is permitted, far beyond what has been known in any other family system, to explore his environment in order to become self-sufficient.

Intense, Open Competition Between Siblings

Because children are equally encouraged to be independent, intense, open competition between siblings ensues. Primogeniture was abolished in the eighteenth century in the United States. In a nation where all are equal, why should first sons have privileges denied other children? Of course, other cultures have competition among siblings, but it is never so openly encouraged as it is in the United States by parental emphasis on the separateness and equality of each child. Everywhere older children resent having to give up the mother's breast to the newborn, but they usually acquire special privileges for having made the sacrifice. Not so in America. Neither age nor sex brings special status. No privileges, favoritism or partiality must be shown any child over and above the others. Because each is encouraged to be independent and is praised for achievement, competition for parental attention and reward is intense and open. What happens is known to every parent in middle-class America, particularly to the mothers. Each child measures for himself the distribution of rewards and punishments given by parents to children. Should Virginia see Harry getting one extra ounce of Coca-Cola, she has several alternatives for action. She can take the case directly to Mom. She can try to sneak something in later in the way of a special favor to make up for her deprivation. She can provoke a fight which puts Harry in the bad. ("He started it and he's bigger.") She may even shove or trip him when no one is looking. Why not? It is a matter of justice.

Prolonged, Agonizing Adolescent Rebellion

There is no feature of American life which releases as much creative or destructive power as the prolonged, agonizing rebellion of American adolescents against their parents. It lasts longer than elsewhere for the American middle-classes because even ten- and eleven-year-olds are encouraged to imitate teenagers and because the majority of twenty- and twenty-one-year-olds have still not entered the world of adult work. It is more agonizing than elsewhere partly because it lasts so long but also because the culture provides so little help to parents and adolescents. With puberty come body changes that throw youth into turmoil everywhere, but nowhere else must an adolescent travel the tortuous path of change from child to adult without so much as a glance at tradition or authority. Mistrusting parental guidance, lacking special roles and responsibilities, it is particularly difficult for the young man or woman to deal with the confusion which develops. With the culture's strong bias against helping the adolescent come to his new identity as adult in terms of family background, he or she is forced into poignant, anguished and often narcissistic introspection. It is a time when "nobody understands me." Parents stumble and careen along a path of inconsistent admonition, criticism and attempted punishment; but the intrusiveness of parents is particularly resented because their authority was compromised long ago.

6 — The Extraordinary Freedom of Unmarried Females

To many outsiders the rebellion of adolescent boys has been more understandable than that of girls. They simply cannot comprehend what is often seen as the most singular feature of the American family system—the extraordinary freedom of unmarried females. In most other countries, independent and unprotected young women bring shame on their families. In most of the world, even today, dependent girls are the nice ones because they are protected; independent, not so nice.

What makes the situation of nubile women in America so different from the rest of the world is that they are the principal architects of their own marriages. Given responsibility for their own mate choice, young Americans invented a remarkable institution still uncopied in most of the world—the unchaperoned date. On her own in dating, the unmarried female in America became practiced at flirting, cajoling and expressing affection while (at least until very recently) holding on to her virginity as the prize for marriage. This did not mean, of course, that she was the equal of young men in initiating courtship, but it usually became her responsibility to regulate the nature and the extent of their sexual experimentation. It was a kind of independence unheard of for respectable girls in most of the rest of the world. Along with such independence went a freedom to travel, initiate conversations with young men and elders and to advertise one's femaleness—behavior seen as bold elsewhere.

The Ambiguity of Male Authority

In the United States, where the ideals of independence and equality held sway, the assertion of the rights of women and children led to an early attack on the traditional authority of fathers and husbands. In a culture which sanctions the rejection of one's family of orientation, encourages precocity and aggressiveness in small children, endorses adolescent rebellion and promotes independence in unmarried females, patriarchy is obsolescent. Moreover, the undermining of male authority in families encourages these other characteristics of the American family. In that sense, the ambiguity of male authority is perhaps the most striking and important characteristic of the American family system.

American culture further undermined male dominance in the home by placing a premium on performance in work outside of it. The pressures to perform on the outside are so great that men often welcome an escape from responsibility and the authority that goes with it at home. The American male today jokes about his condition in television serials, comic strips (where married men are depicted as weak, confused and even stupid) and in after-dinner stories, and is seemingly helpless to do anything about it. In response to family problems he often throws up his hands; he burrows his head in the newspapers; he plays golf with the boys; or he plunges further into work. He can help with the chores (particularly if he is in the classic Anglo-Saxon mold, where it is virtuous to be handy and work around the house) or he can play with the kids (relieve some of Mom's tension and escape from his pressures into more childlike activity), but in middle-class America, now more than ever, his authority is often doubted and rarely felt.

The Power and Assertiveness of Married Women

A visitor from Scotland investigating the conditions of laborers in the United States in the middle of the nineteenth century, although sympathetic to the assertiveness of working men on the job, was distraught to see the crippling of male authority at home. Astonished to find that middle-class husbands even did some of the "slip-slop" work, he blamed the condition on the bossiness of their wives. His view was oversimplified, but other foreigners and immigrants too, frequently have written and spoken of this eighth characteristic of the American family system, the power and assertiveness of married women.

How dare any man talk of the power of married females at the very time when both men and women are recognizing not only that there is sharp discrimination against women in employment, but also that women continue to bear a much larger responsibility than men for child-rearing, the preparation of meals and the maintenance of the household generally? But that is precisely one of the points to be made. Someone has to make decisions in families, and in the United States the responsibility for governing American households on a day-to-day basis has fallen largely on the women. It may be a responsibility which some wives would want their husbands to assume. But that is not the issue here. The empirical fact is that in American families the degree to which women have more real decision-making authority than their husbands is greater than that almost anywhere else. They have considerable economic power, since a huge proportion of family decisions has to do with spending money; they have religious power because they bear almost entirely the responsibility for the moral and religious guidance of the young; and they even have the power to break up their families while maintaining considerable protection for themselves through unusual divorce laws. Reinforcing these manifestations of power has been the power to earn money in the marketplace, thus reducing economic dependence on fathers and husbands.

It is the alleged assertiveness much more than power which is complained about by men. As the Scotch visitor noticed, husbands grumble at what they see as undue assertiveness, which is something less and yet more than decision-making power. American women have been depicted as pushing their husbands and families toward success, admonishing males for bad behavior and competing against each other for both family status and personal recognition. Europeans and Asians have watched with astonishment as American women openly scold their husbands or extravagantly boast of their small children.

The Anxieties of Mothering

What is called assertiveness may be in part a manifestation of underlying anxiety. The anxieties of mothering in
the United States results from many factors. Certainly,
the burden of making and enforcing decisions in democratic households brings considerable pressure on American mothers. It is not just that decision-making has shifted
to mothers; in America, she has very little help from her
own parents, and is not even sure that she wants it, or
from aunts, cousins, older siblings or servants. Tradition
is no help; change is the law of life in America, where she
is told that to be a good mother she must keep up with
the newest, latest and best methods and equipment for
child-rearing. To assist her, she eagerly purchases popular journals giving advice on mothering, as she has done
ever since the early nineteenth century. She watches the
advice of experts avidly. For one generation it is Watson;
for the next two, Spock. When the marketplace offers a
plurality of expert opinions, as it often does, she chooses
anxiously among them. If she is lucky, she will have a husband who helps with the baby-sitting, diapers and dishes,
but it is she who feels the responsibility.

Preparing the young for achievement through competition means watching their health, supervising their
choice of friends and encouraging them in schoolwork.
For in America, children even of humble origins can, with
the right guidance and influence, grow up to become presidents of corporations, universities and the nation itself.
Even when mothers are not so concerned about achieve-

ment, they are aware through exposure to Freud and psychology that they carry a terrifying responsibility for the future happiness and well-being of their children.

In the meantime, mother must cope with the precocity, aggressiveness, competition and rebellion which the culture promotes among her brood. It is the mother and not the father who usually bears the day-to-day task of countering their disrespect. If the children imprison her, she still dares not think of them—source of pride, joy and love—as tyrants. If anxiety overwhelms her and depression follows, she is more likely to turn either inward on herself or against her husband.

Middle-class mothers also are likely to feel a keen sense of anxiety about not using their brains to the fullest. Their frustration at being cut off from other people or from artistically and intellectually creative activities may be complicated by a sense of guilt at not being "a good-enough mother" when they become preoccupied about their own self-development.

Intensifying the anxieties of mothers is the pressure in America for middle-aged women to remain attractive, if not alluring. At the very least, the married woman wants to be a married mistress; at most, she wants attention from and flirtations with other men. Again, she has reason to feel guilty as a mother. But perhaps the anxiety stems not so much from the guilt as from the actual fear of losing one's attractiveness in the more-than-twenty-year career of mothering which brings the average woman close to menopause. The mother and wife in her fifties, looking back and seeing lost opportunities for her personal development, may be preoccupied with new lines in her face, bulges that have appeared recently and a feeling that her energy is flagging. From the media, and especially from powerful advertising, she learns that in America only the young are thought to be beautiful.

The Embarrassments of Growing Old

Growing old is not associated with pleasure in the United States as it is in so many other cultures. It brings no distinctions, favors, privileges or power. The American way of aging leads to the last of the ten distinctive characteristics, the embarrassments of growing old. The pains of aging in the United States are much more psychological than physical. Nowhere else has so much been done to help people live longer; nowhere else is so little done to help them live longer gracefully and with dignity. In a nation which celebrates youth and change, the old are not only cut off from power and privilege but even from the pleasure which comes when young men and women openly appreciate how much they owe to past generations.

But the main crime of the very old is that they have become dependent and are no longer productive. In traditional societies particularly, where individual achievement has meant little and group harmony much, the failure of the old to be productive in American terms would not be counted against them. Their knowledge of traditions and wisdom at interpreting them makes them valuable contributors to society until their death. Because dependency is recognized as valuable and healthy, even their physical dependency is not resented unless, as is true in a few cases, the shortage of food is extreme. Even in such cases, the old die with the respect of the young. Millions of the old in America do come to terms with aging and dying, but nowhere else is the process as psychologically debilitating.

The American-ness of It All

The picture of aging in America is bleak and perhaps over-simplified; each of these concepts about the American family system has been presented starkly without much qualification. That is because I want Americans to appreciate much more than they do how culturally determined are their own family situations. Valuing so highly the individual against society, Americans are reluctant to believe that their values, attitudes and behavior are culturally formed. They hate to be lumped together by a generalization. Even if America were not made up of many subcultures living in a vast land, there would be individuals or families who are exceptions to every feature of the system described here. It should be clear at the outset that I am *generalizing* about a large majority of middle-class families in America. It is the middle-class family system that has been written about by American dramatists, novelists and poets for more than a hundred years and which is now presented daily and nightly on television.

It should also be clear that while the family system had its origins in the eighteenth and nineteenth centuries, it has been more sharply defined in the twentieth. The emphasis given to independence and equality in American families is more pronounced than ever for several reasons: the ideals have gained greater force; the middle classes keep expanding despite the persistence of miserable poverty for some Americans (according to census statistics, a diminishing proportion); the spill of affluence has made possible more numerous choices for larger numbers of women and children; and technological developments—from automation to the pill—have blurred traditional distinctions in roles and functions between men and women. Wherever these factors are present, as they are among the urban upper-middle classes in the cities of Europe, many features of the American middle-class family system have emerged.

In what sense, then, can that system be called "American"? In the sense that it emerged first in the United States and has been the dominant system there for a long time on farms and in small towns as well as in cities. Also, only in the United States have these ten interrelated characteristics emerged as a result of a political ideology emphasizing personal independence and equality. Finally, it can be shown that while other societies—traditional or modern—may exhibit one or more aspects of the American family system, nowhere else does the combination of characteristics stemming from the quest for independence and equality appear as an integrated system. Precocious children abounded in ancient Rome; unmarried women of eighteen in a socialist Israeli kibbutz have much freedom; the married women of modern Russia certainly are assertive; there is considerable ambiguity of male authority in the Hopi Indian family, as there often is in matrilineal families; the literature of Victorian England oozed sentimentality about the family of procreation. But nowhere do these characteristics of family life appear together as an integral system except in the United States. Nowhere else are they related to the ceaseless, relentless struggle for personal salvation. When they do appear in other societies, they are likely to emerge in a completely different context. For example, young Japanese children are spoiled and show considerable precocity. Yet, their behavior and their elders' attitude toward them have nothing to do with the ideals of independence and equality. Their behavior is set in a special stage of life in which young children are indulged prior to moving into another phase.

The American family system is tied to the democratic ideal of equality. The first meaning of that ideal to most Americans has been equal opportunity for white males to succeed through work and to participate in the political process. With the growth of abundance and the extension of that ideal, that goal of equal opportunity in work and politics has been applied increasingly to women and dark-skinned Americans. Another meaning of the egalitarian ideal has been the assertion of the rights of children and women against traditional patriarchal society in families. The results have not been without irony. In Asian countries where lower-class or caste men have had virtually no opportunity to rise to higher status through achievement, aristocratic women have held important positions (both India and Ceylon have had female prime ministers in recent years). In America, where white males of poor backgrounds have been encouraged to have high ambition, even superbly educated women have not aspired to positions of unusual distinction or power outside of the home but have taken on much of the responsibility for household governance that in other cultures belongs to males. My American students were astonished a few years ago when, in a seminar on the family, a graduate student from Thailand reported that her mother was a full professor in the department where her father held a junior rank. "How could that be? Wouldn't he be terribly upset?" the Americans asked with raised eyebrows. She answered, "Why should he be upset? Mother is superb in her field. Besides, when he comes home in the evening, he is still her husband. Dinner is served just the way he wants it, when he wants it, and proper respect is paid to him as father and husband." My Thai student could have added that she was speaking for a way of life in Asia that is possible for only a tiny percentage of the people, the upper classes. There upper-class women can organize household work with the help of servants and family while they pursue educational, professional and even governmental careers usually available only to men in the egalitarian United States. In Thailand, no less than in America, the family system is tied to the class system and both are shaped by the dominant values of the culture.

WE ARE IN IT TOGETHER

The main point of this book, then, is that what is seen as the war between the generations or between the sexes in the United States is part of a family system with deep cultural roots. Whether or not you accept my generalizations as descriptive of the middle-class American family, you may see this version of American families as dismal. I am writing not to praise or disparage the American family system but to try to understand and communicate about it.

While I see anxiety, loneliness and new kinds of conflicts as the price Americans have paid for independence and equality in families, I believe there have been enormous benefits, too. One has only to see the envy of many European and Asian girls of the freedom which American young men and women have to appreciate that the American idea of independence holds something of real value. Love shared through an adult lifetime of conflict-and-reconciliation between a man and a woman who chose each other is an ideal which is becoming increasingly attractive in many parts of the world at the very time that Americans are raising questions about it. The liberation of women and children from the subjugation characteristic of many patriarchal and rigidly double-standard societies has brought happiness to them and has released creative talent for society. The American family system is good *and* bad in human terms. What is bad or good depends on your opinion of the emotional and spiritual needs of men and women. It is a question of your version of the good life. What is important is not that American families are better or worse than others. It is that they are different. It is my view that understanding how and why they are different may help individuals to become better spouses, parents and children. At least, it may help them to understand that what is happening to them is not unique but in part is a result of powerful cultural forces.

My plea is not for the American way or the Thai family system. It is to reduce the rhetoric of antagonism between generations and the sexes. There is much conflict and tension, but few conspirators or enemies. The old and the men are on the defensive; the young and the women are attacking. While the vast majority of Americans are not yet nearly as angry as the most militant among the attackers, there is not much hope for constructive change unless we pause to consider how we got where we are and where we are heading, unless we look honestly at our own sacred cow—independence and equality in American families.

II In the Kingdom of the Young

W. C. Fields, who knew what really mattered in America, was fond of saying that anyone who hated dogs and little children couldn't be all bad. The more typical American view, particularly since the nineteenth century, has been that the young are more important and virtuous than the old. All other major cultures have viewed the young as untrustworthy; they must be civilized by society, prepared for responsible membership in it, and defer to the wisdom of their elders. The Chinese probably provided the sharpest contrast to the American point of view. Their aged were revered; children had no rights at all. The term of endearment for one's wife was *tai-tai* (great-grand), not "baby" or "chick." Jokes were made about awkward and embarrassed sons-in-law, not mothers-in-law.

THE NEW IS BETTER THAN THE OLD

A civilization's view of the old and the young is very much influenced by its picture of the past and the future. America was founded on hopes for the future. To most early Americans, the past meant Europe, and Europe, at best, was antiquated; at worst, it was corrupt. The characteristic American greeting, "What's new?," tells what interests Americans. The manufacturers and advertisers know so well the bias of Americans for newness that they plan obsolescence in automobiles, put ineffectual ingredients in soaps and detergents in order to claim that the product is new, and even regenerate standard successful products through new packaging or new slogans. The attitude toward newness underlies both the rejection of the family of orientation and the idealization of the family of procreation. Because Americans have tended to think that change means progress, they have no impulse to revere the family from which they come. Because they have had —until now—almost unlimited confidence that they could make the future better than the past, they have tended to idealize the future of families which they start for themselves.

HOW PRECIOUS THE SEED!

Americans became early marriers in the seventeenth century for economic reasons, but by the late eighteenth century they were also marrying early for the same reasons as they are now: to get away from home, to have socially approved sex, to fulfill one's ideals and to have babies. Children represent the future, and Americans want to get on with it. Thus American children are born into an environment which not only welcomes them but which puts extraordinary trust and hope in them. In the late eighteenth century, Thomas Jefferson enunciated a principle which was becoming an American ideal—that each generation should consider itself "as a distinct nation, with a right, by the will of its majority, to bind themselves, but none to bind the succeeding generation, more than they have the right to bind the inhabitants of another country." Jefferson's doctrine would have shocked the Puritan governors of New England and the plantation Cavaliers of his own Virginia a hundred and fifty years before; but even then powerful forces were pushing children toward assertive and precocious behavior much more rapidly than those elsewhere.

The reasons were both religious and economic. Indeed children in early Puritan America were not allowed to be children. The Puritan view can be summed up as follows. To save my child's immortal soul, his impulse for pleasure must be curbed. He must learn how to assume responsibility and how to work hard. The best antidote to lust, laziness and white lies was hard work. Work was not only the best protection against the devil and the terrors of hell, but it was also the best preparation for a virtuous life. Moreover, every hand was needed to maintain the homestead. Girls of six could spin flax. Boys could bring in fuel, cut seed, water horses, pick berries, gather vegetables and feed the pigs. There was sawing and wood-chopping to do. Children of both sexes could sow seeds, weed flax fields and comb wool. A busy child not only was kept from mischief which threatened his soul, and received training to compete in the adult work, but actually made his father's farm more productive.

Because Protestantism emphasized the importance of the Scriptures, it was necessary for children to learn to read. By 1649, some degree of education was compulsory in every New England colony except Rhode Island. Children of three were sometimes taught to read Latin words as well as English. Boys as young as six and a half entered Boston Latin School. Education and work both promoted early responsibility. Girl orphans were permitted to choose their own guardians at fourteen. Governor John Winthrop of the Massachusetts Bay Colony made his son of fourteen the executor of his will, and until the American Revolution boys of sixteen paid taxes and served in the militia.

None of this is meant to suggest that Puritan families were permissive. While responsibility was encouraged, independence of children was not applauded. Many believed it was a sin for children to complain about their parents. Corporal punishment was liberally employed through birch rods, canes, leather straps and humiliating devices such as the dunce cap. But by stressing self-sufficiency, the Puritan fathers subverted their own authority. In 1657 the Reverend Ezekiel Rogers wrote that he found "greatest trouble and grief about the rising generation. Young people . . . strengthen one another in evil by example and by counsel." Then, in a lament familiar to parents of each succeeding generation, he complained, "Much ado have I with my own family." By the early eighteenth century, many parents complained of difficulty in controlling children. The influential preacher Jonathan Edwards observed in his home city of Northampton, Massachusetts, that parents were permitting their children amusements, visiting and late hours on the grounds that children of others were permitted excesses. So began the child's plea, "Mom, Fred's mother lets him do it." Enforcing the rules became difficult in the face of laxity by others. Children also began to challenge the privileges of older siblings, and open warfare between them became commonplace. Judge Samuel Sewell complained in his diary in 1692 that his son threw a brass knob and hit his sister on the forehead so as to make it bleed and swell.

LITTLE CHILDREN ARE SEEN AND HEARD

How does a child become self-sufficient without asserting the self? In America, where the egalitarian ideal was taking hold, there seemed to be no other way. Seventeenth- and eighteenth-century parents wondered what they could do about the younger generation. A seventeenth-century plaint runs, "What little hope of a happy generation after us, when many among us scarcely know how to keep their children managed!" By the early nineteenth century, European visitors to America thought that the situation was entirely out of hand.

It was then that childhood precocity became a marked feature of American life. The erosion of parental authority—particularly that of the father—apparently caused by the unimpeded precocity, impudence and energy of American children, was observed by dozens of visiting foreigners. But which came first: the ambiguity of paternal authority or the aggressiveness of the young, the chicken or the egg? One can find in any good library of Americana at least three dozen comments comparable to the remarks of a visitor who said that it was not to be wondered at that "boys assumed the airs of full-grown cockscombs . . . when most parents make it a principle never to check [them] . . ." With horror he observed boys from well-to-do families shouting and swearing in the public streets. Uniformly, visitors found parental indulgence to be responsible for the unkempt behavior of children. They were shocked to see young girls convulsed in anger at their parents without being reproved. Faces went dirty and hair uncombed.

The first half of the nineteenth century, particularly, saw marked changes in the feeding and other child-rearing practices of American parents. Some infants were permitted to feed themselves from a cup at an unusually early age. At ten to fifteen months small children would be seated at the family dinner table in high chairs, where, according to foreigners, their behavior was especially astounding. As soon as the child could sit at the table, he chose his own food, and as one Englishwoman wrote, bickered with his parents about manners and eating habits. As for clothing, the child-rearing literature of the period favored loose garments to encourage freedom of movement for the infant.

Many parents complained of the irreverence of the young, but some of them encouraged it. Parents often would dote on their children rather than discipline them for impudent behavior. Visitors would be shown the pictures of children and told all about them. No bows or curtsies on introduction, but a straightforward look in the eye and a cordial handshake as if the child were a grownup. One European noted, even "sensible people smile with secret admiration" at the rebelliousness of their offspring. A Polish count summed it up in 1857 by observing that parents allowed an almost unlimited choice to their children. One couple observed that they were permitted to roam around the house, "circulating freely like little birds." The mother, it was observed, had them under her eye but not under control. For the children had their own way, "tumbling and dragging about books and cushions and chairs and climbing up and down just as they pleased."

EDUCATION FOR PERSONAL ACHIEVEMENT

While parents, ministers and teachers complained about the rudeness of their children, there does not seem to have been any recognition that there was a relationship between the aggressive behavior of the young and the emphasis of their parents on personal achievement as a way of promoting self-sufficiency. Pushing the infant and small child toward achievement became the American way in the early nineteenth century. Infants were sometimes required to sit up before they were able. During the 1830's dozens of women's magazines and manuals for child care appeared which encouraged parents to promote the curiosity of the young through nature study and other educational activities. In the following decade the rapidly expanding free elementary school systems of the New England states, Pennsylvania, Ohio and New York took up the cause of achievement through competition. The ideal of independence through achievement reached even the schoolchildren of parents who did not believe in it (such as Irish or German immigrants) via McGuffy's *Readers.* Be independent and achieving, said the *Readers,* and yes, obey your parents too. But the schools subverted parental authority by the main message preached in one of the *Readers,* whose third edition in 1853 reminded children that "in this free community, there are no privileged orders. Every man must find his level." "If you are talented and work hard," said the most influential schoolbook in American history, "you are bound to get ahead in America."

Sometimes fathers subverted parental authority too. Having lost to their wives the main responsibility and authority for disciplining their children, some applauded disobedience in the young as a proper sign of independence and aggressiveness, particularly for the boys. This became particularly true in the latter half of the nineteenth century. In John Hayes's popular poem, "Little

Breeches" (1871), a father proudly describes his four-year-old son as "pert and chipper and sassy, always ready to swear and fight..."

The retreat from discipline advocated in the articles of the *Ladies Home Journal* in the 1880's and 1890's was probably related to the growing cult of personal independence. It was urged that children be allowed to lead their own lives. They were plants, each with individual growth tendencies—a little water, nourishment, and let them go their own way. Most astoundingly, they were listened to by parents as if small boys or girls were equal in judgment and capacity to grownups.

THE GREAT AMERICAN DISCIPLINE DEBATE

At the very time that children were permitted intimacies of the household where they could learn to imitate the ways of adults, their own literature—designed to give fantasies full play—virtually excluded adults. Boys and girls sought their own fortunes, planned their own enterprises (in the style of Horatio Alger), and even drove railway trains and steamboats and managed farms. The universal hero was Tom Sawyer (the book was first published in 1876), who stole from and outsmarted his Aunt Polly, misbehaved in church, and bragged his way through a self-sufficient idyllic boyhood. Aunt Polly knew she should be more strict but somehow she just could not.

The great debate in American child-rearing literature of the twentieth century—as in the past—is over the issue of permissiveness versus discipline. Broadly speaking, there have been two main reasons why American parents have been preoccupied with that question. The first is that training for self-reliance, which encourages children to make choices for themselves, sometimes conflicts not just with the desire to protect children but with training for achievement which requires the self-control and discipline that can come from setting limits and enforcing them.

The second reason is the American inheritance of Protestant (and to some extent Jansenistic Catholic*) asceticism, which in its extreme expression holds that pleasure is sinful and further maintains that pleasure can interfere with independence and impede achievement. The anti-pleasure principle applied to the child runs head-on into the disposition of parents to indulge the precocity of their children.

To judge from child-rearing literature since the 1940's, the American ascetic legacy has atrophied considerably. It is no longer widely believed that pleasure in children is sinful or leads to sin, or that independence and achievement will be sharply curbed by good fun. Whereas the 1914 Infant Care Bulletin of the Children's Bureau of the United States Department of Labor urged mothers to be vigilant in protecting the child from dangerous masturbatory and sucking impulses, the infant care bulletins issued since 1942 legitimize the baby's pleasurable actions.

---

* Jansenism, eventually declared a heresy by the Roman Catholic Church, stressed the depravity of natural human instincts, especially the sexual. It was a significant factor in the Irish Church in the late eighteenth and early nineteenth centuries because the Jansenist priests who fled France in the decades following the French Revolution staffed the seminary at Maynooth in Ireland. The primary influence in America was, of course, Calvinism.

What in 1914 were wicked propensities, which would in-
duce dependency, have become normal tendencies which
infants and children should be allowed to explore in order
to develop their individual personalities.

In recent decades the argument over strictness versus
permissiveness has rested on the issue of what is best for
self-sufficiency and achievement. In the 1930's child-rearing literature still talked of independence mainly in terms
of *self-discipline* and achievement. By the 1960's, under
the influence of Freud and other schools of psychological
thought, child-rearing literature spoke of independence in
terms of *self-expression* and achievement. The most influential child-care expert of the 1930's was the prominent
American behaviorist John B. Watson, who, in his *Psychological Care of Infant and Child* (1928), prescribed one
classic American formula for self-discipline and achievement. He told mothers to keep their emotional distance
from their children and to give them a series of tasks to
accomplish. Overresponsiveness to the child's cries for
food or attention will generally make them dependent, he
warned. Don't coddle, kiss or fondle. Such affection and
attention, he said, would not only make the children "dependent" but would limit their capacities in "conquering
the world." In order to conquer the world, have them
master their feeding schedules, toilet training and other
infant tasks according to a strict regimen. At the end of
his book, Watson wrote that the child who can cope
with the demands of American society will be "as free as
possible of sensitivities to people and one who, almost
from birth, is relatively independent of the family situa-

tion . . . we have tried to create a problem-solving technique . . . plus boundless absorption in activity . . ."

Watson's behaviorism was followed by middle-class mothers during the thirties but declined in the forties and fifties as its pseudo-scientific basis fell and the ascetic ideal against pleasure declined. Self-expression increasingly became an important measure of the independence of infants and children. Permissiveness with respect to infant feeding, crawling, walking and even (to a lesser extent) toilet training and (to a still lesser extent) sexual play became common in middle-class families.

Replacing Watson as the principal mother's guide to child-rearing was Dr. Benjamin Spock, whose *Baby and Child Care*, first published in 1945, advised against Watson's rigid prescriptions for independence training. Dr. Spock urged a flexible or what-feels-comfortable approach to child-rearing—a dash of permissiveness here, some strictness there. In the earliest editions of his famous book he warned against too much strictness. Later, he worried that a conscientious parent might get into trouble with permissiveness, too. On the independence issue Spock has been fundamentally consistent. American infants and children have to be helped to "wean themselves from their dependence." In addition, they need a chance to do things on their own. The child "needs space to run and shout in, apparatus to climb on, blocks and boards to build with, trains and dolls to play with . . . to think up projects and work them out. . . ." Spock-reared children, no less than those raised under the tutelage of Watson, are still expected to satisfy society's demands for individual independence and achievement. According to European and Asian observers, contemporary American children remain notorious for their self-centeredness, assertiveness and precocity.

ACHIEVE, ACHIEVE! (AND ENJOY?)

According to parents the way to express independence is still through a series of achievements. The middle classes push their children as much as before. Many middle-class mothers rush their children into nursery school so that they can learn to be on their own and develop proper social and motor skills. There are obviously many good reasons in a highly mobile, competitive society for children to go to nursery school, and there is the very good reason of having fun, too. An additional good reason is that the precocity and aggressiveness of small children is exhausting for mom. The nursery school—like the television set—becomes important not only because the child must learn to be free from mother, but because mom has to be free from the tension of her relationships with her children. Let the child turn some of his energy onto his playmates and teacher or let him identify with the adventures of TV's newest great achievers. Many parents realistically and understandably dread the summer vacation when classes end and the best TV programs are suspended, and if they can afford it, send their pre-teen children to summer camp, where every achievement from passing the deep-end test to learning how to dance with members of the opposite sex at age eight receives parental approval.

American children in the eighteenth and nineteenth centuries were anxious to act as adults do. Today, if we are to judge by their television programs and popular games, they are more in a hurry than ever. At the same time that affluence makes achievement through work less inviting, it makes achievement through imitation of adult play and social relations not only more accessible but more necessary to fill the gap left by the disappearance of real tasks.

A perfect illustration of this kind of precocity as applied to the independent, unmarried female can be seen in America's all-time successful doll, the "Barbie Hi-Fashion Doll," which, from 1959 until recently (it has had more than a decade of success), took little girls from five to twelve into the fantasy world of teenage utopia. Barbie, successor to the infant dolls of previous generations and the Shirley Temple dolls of the thirties, is built like a healthy, athletic American woman of twenty, although the Barbie game and literature place her age more nearly at sixteen. Barbie and all her accessories constituted a business of more than fifty million dollars annually in the sixties.

For the ultimate in precocity, see the Barbie game entitled "Barbie, Queen of the Prom," most often played by girls under ten. To become Queen of the Prom, a player has to achieve four other victories. She must be elected president of a club, win a boyfriend, be asked by him to go steady, and earn or find enough money to be able to buy an expensive prom dress. The last is not as hard as it used to be. In the game little Barbie players do not make a move without getting paid for it. If they wash the dinner dishes, they collect a dollar. Walking the neighbor's dog earns a couple of dollars. If they type letters for dad, they get paid four dollars, presumably at a dollar a letter. A more disagreeable job—correcting test papers for the teacher—earns six dollars. Bigger money can be had as a fashion model. A girl also receives money without working (a five-dollar allowance every time she passes home and a ten-dollar gift certificate from dad when he receives an extra large stock dividend). She also might get to use her girlfriend's sports car. The friend has just gone to Europe.

Barbie never gives anything away, but when she finds a wallet she collects five dollars. When her girlfriend's sister asks her to address invitations to a wedding, she picks up two more. She needs that money because dresses are expensive. The least costly one, called Silken Flame, costs thirty-five dollars (extremely expensive in 1960), but if Barbie is lucky enough, she will be able to purchase "Enchanted Evening" at sixty-five dollars. Barbie has additional expenses when she lands on the spaces marked "Soda Fountain," "Sweet Shop," "Beauty Shop" or in "School." There she must pay three dollars for a lost textbook and absorb other penalties.

She can go steady with one of four boys. They are important to Barbie but not as persons. She needs them to get to the prom. A "surprise" card tells the lucky player: "You are voted the most popular girl in your class. If you need one, you may choose any boyfriend who is not taken, or, you may exchange your present boyfriend (unless he is your steady date) for any boyfriend not yet taken." The boys do not amount to much. We learn nothing about Tom. Poindexter receives ten dollars for writing a poem which is printed in the newspaper and insists on giving Barbie half. (Would Barbie have done the same for him?) Bob has trouble spelling and is coached by one of the girl players, and Ken runs out of gas on a date. The boyfriend, like the club presidency and expensive dress, is a stepping stone on the way to bigger things. Any eight-year-old can play and become queen of the prom in a fifty-dollar formal black-sequinned gown appropriately called Solo in the Spotlight.

Why is Barbie worth so much discussion? Because Barbie is more typical of independent, unmarried teenage females, even in the 1970's, than more sophisticated girls her age who are thinking about living in communes. Statistics tell us that Barbie will be married by the time she is nineteen and give birth to her last child when she is twenty-five or -six (her more educated and sophisticated American sisters will wait longer).

Barbie's precocity will not take her to sensitivity training groups and she probably will not read Hesse or Vonnegut, but the Barbies of America still constitute a majority in the middle classes. She is a twentieth-century variation on an old theme, the effervescent, high-spirited, young American who won't be bridled by anyone. Hawthorne gave little Pearl an "uncontrollable will" in *The Scarlet Letter*. Huck Finn felt "clamped-up and smothery" at home but "free and easy on a raft." More recently, Thornton Wilder made it clear in *Our Town* that parents in

America have to negotiate with or pay their children for cooperation. Barbie is an all-American girl.

What makes her so attractive to eight- and nine-year-olds is precisely that they imagine the teenage world to be free of parental control. They may not yet know how miserable the kings and queens can be in the kingdom of the young. Adolescence is a time of breaking away from parental authority, and from the vantage point of the pre-teenager, that looks mighty exciting.

ON BEING AN AMERICAN ADOLESCENT

Why is a protracted adolescent rebellion against authority so particularly American when the culture already has given the young so much freedom? One obvious answer is that having known considerable freedom, they tend to resist any effort to limit it, especially when they are struggling for self-definition in adolescence.

In all cultures, each new generation must find a way to enter adulthood. What makes the passage so long and agonizing for American youths is that they must make the journey on their own. Puberty brings chaotic physical and psychological changes; yet, in the United States there are no puberty rites, no special economic functions set aside for youth, no special roles, and no formal initiation into sex by one's elders. The chaos of adolescence demands structure, support and affection, and resisting parental intrusiveness, the young seek them from each other. Striving for recognition as adults, they rebel against their parents. What is felt by parents to be rebellion is for adolescents an assertion of their desire for independence

For girls, the declaration of independence against parents is frequently shown in sexual behavior. That is probably more true now than ever. In the twentieth century many factors, beginning in the 1920's, combined to make early sex relations a way of declaring independence and fighting the older generation: spending money, automobiles, contraceptives and the advertisement of sexuality in merchandising and movies. By the 1960's, 40 percent of America's ten- and eleven-year-old girls and 60 percent of the thirteen- and fourteen-year-olds went out on dates. Popular teenage lipsticks went by the names of Come Closer Honey, Sugar Daddy Red, Yes, Yes Pink, Nearly Nude and Orange Gone Wild.

The declaration of independence for boys has less to do with sex than it does for girls because parents are less anxious about their boys' sexual conduct. Rebellion is asserted by doing poorly in school, talking back to one's parents, ignoring them or going wherever and with whomever one wants behind the wheel of an automobile. If there is a rite of adolescence in the United States, it is getting an automobile license. To the boy, especially, the automobile represents those things which matter most in American life: energy; mastery; achievement; mobility; and, above all, the independence these give.

Nowhere is the conflict between independence training and parental concern (control or intrusiveness from the teenagers' point of view) more obvious than in the bickering which goes on over the use of the family car. The experience, ability and judgment of young men behind the wheel are, on average, clearly inferior to those of their fathers. Yet, the ideals of independence and equality encourage fathers to share the car with their sometimes reckless sons. Mom and dad may sit at home and talk about his recklessness, resent it and be troubled by it, but they are not always certain what to do about it. Many adults are uncomfortable about the narcissistic spontaneity of teenagers. The words one most often hears are "selfish," "thoughtless" and "irresponsible." It is precisely because of and not despite the American celebration of youth that their energy, health, sexual verve and irreverence are often resented. Where such qualities are not valued as much as experience, age and power, there is no need to be envious.

ADOLESCENT LONELINESS

The young may be envied by their elders, but adolescence in America is increasingly a time of acute loneliness. Because the adolescent is self-absorbed in the struggle for identity and intimacy, parents see him as self-centered—unplanned, inefficient, not punctual and unresponsive—and are often unsympathetic in reacting to the turbulence of his feelings. Thus, the teenager, ostensibly wanting distance from his parents, gets it. Parents not wanting it, find it difficult to close the gap. When they try, the teenager often resents their intrusion and feels even more alone in his search for identity and love.

The belief that one can find one's identity and overcome loneliness through love is not new in America. The lyrics of popular songs from the 1890's on promise that romance between boy and girl is an effective antidote for

personal loneliness. What is new about more recent popular songs and teenage literature is the awareness by adolescents of their loneliness as a group and their deep
pessimism despite their hopes for love. Even before the
talent of the Beatles and Bob Dylan made itself felt, the
songs of the early sixties dwelled on adolescent independence, loneliness and love. Typical were "Leader of the
Pack" (parents breaking up a teenage marriage), "King
of the Road" (always on the move, even out of a trailer
camp where rooms can be rented for fifty cents), "I Know
a Place" or "Downtown" (to get away from parents),
"New York Is a Lonely Town" (the loneliness theme)
and "Follow the Sun" (unrequited love). Then came the
Beatles, Dylan, and Simon and Garfunkel, the poets of
the generation who came to consciousness in the 1960's.
They were sharply critical of the older generation. Their
songs stressed the hypocrisy of society, the loneliness of
the good person against society and the evils of social
injustice. They constituted not just a manifesto of rebellion but an admission of loneliness and confusion, as
when Dylan tells us that his existence is tied to "confusion boats."

The new music of the sixties was compatible with the
teenage folk hero of the late fifties Holden Caulfield, the
boy in J.D. Salinger's *The Catcher in the Rye*. A completely new teenage hero, Holden sought independence
(as did Huck Finn, Tom Sawyer and the Horatio Alger
heroes), but unlike them, life for him was complexly
painful and lonely. Here was a sixteen-year-old with
whom teenagers could identify. He had a distant father,

about whose work and income he knew little ("He's never discussed that stuff with me . . ."), and an anxious mother ("She's nervous as hell"). He hated dishonesty, was terribly lonely, and wanted more than anything else to love and be loved. As for goals, why bother?

In the mid-sixties, Holden grew into Benjamin of Mike Nichol's *The Graduate*. Estranged from his parents and their friends, put off by opportunities in the business world, discouraged by the pressure to achieve, disgusted with himself for not knowing what he wanted to do, and for failing to work out a satisfactory love relationship, Benjamin was as depressed as Holden was, even though he was at least six years older. Benjamin's condition was echoed in the film by the lyrics and music of Simon and Garfunkel, who chided Mrs. Robinson for her hypocrisy, society for its neon gods and its failure to love. Following their success in *The Graduate*, Simon and Garfunkel continued to cut records which, like the Beatles' before them, sensitively interpreted the feelings of adolescents in rebellion. In 1970 they replaced the disbanded Beatles and the relatively inactive Bob Dylan as the poets of adolescence with a new hit record called "Bridge Over Troubled Water." Within six months of its release it had sold three million copies. The main themes were loneliness and love. In "Why Don't You Write Me" Paul Simon pleaded that a letter would brighten his lonely evening even if it only said "that you are leaving me."

Parents who think it is impossible to learn what their teenagers are feeling and thinking should listen to the records they are buying, or they should turn their radio dials to a music station that caters to the teenage market. Music has become incredibly big business in the United States. (Record sales alone climbed from five hundred million in 1960 (the beginning of the twist) to more than 1.2 billion in 1970.) Of course, not all teenagers, not even within the white middle classes, are listening to the same music. The more sophisticated respond to themes of alienation, explicit sex, social injustice and even nostalgic history. But those groups and songs with widest appeal dwell on the tension between loneliness and love.

In their earliest songs the Beatles told simply and almost innocently of love's healing powers. Loneliness and love are the twin themes in "All I've Got to Do," "Anytime at All," "All My Lovin'," "P.S. I Love You," "And I Love Her," "Eight Days a Week" and many more. The Beatles looked at ways other than love to overcome loneliness and found them wanting—work (in "A Hard Day's Night"); conformity to the crowd (in "Nowhere Man"); and quick sex ("Day Tripper")—although one can escape loneliness through drugs, or seem to, and have some fantastic highs ("A Day in the Life" or "Lucy in the Sky with Diamonds"). In some of their later songs the Beatles became more pessimistic about the curative powers of love. Loneliness, alienation and sheer misery appeared to be the human condition. In "Strawberry Fields Forever" they sang of nothing being real and of "misunderstanding doing all you see." In "Eleanor Rigby" they looked at all the lonely people and concluded that "no one was saved." Yet, like Holden in *The Catcher in the Rye* and Benjamin in *The Graduate*, they kept coming back to love between two persons—"All You Need Is Love"—as the way to get together with yourself and the world.

⟨In the late sixties the more terrifying aspects of the Beatles' music found popular expression in a new kind of blues through Janis Joplin and in acid rock through Jimi Hendrix. When Joplin sang that love was just a "Ball and Chain" and that "freedom's just another word for nothing to lose," or when thousands stomped and screamed at Hendrix singing "Manic-Depression," large numbers of young people blatantly advertised their own depression. Later, in 1970, James Taylor returned again to the theme of love in tender, introspective songs which appealed more to marijuana smokers than to those who took hallucinogens or harder drugs. But with all of the spokesmen for youth—Holden, Benjamin, the Beatles, Dylan, Simon and Garfunkel, Joplin, Hendrix and even James Taylor—there is not much love to be found in the world of adults. Becoming an adult is a bleak prospect. The age of hard rock or acid rock may be over; but the unhappiness of youth which helped to produce it has not ended.⟩

AWARENESS-OVERLOAD

Some of the critics of youth may shake their heads in disbelief to read of the unhappiness of the young. Why should the generation that came to consciousness in the 1960's be particularly depressed when they have it so good? But clearly, a sense of well-being does not come from increased purchasing power. Nor does it necessarily come from greater independence.

For many in that generation the decade began with the assassination of John F. Kennedy. (The Beatles had not yet cut their first record in the United States.) Then there were the killings of Medgar Evers, Malcolm X, Martin Luther King and Robert Kennedy; constant social strife; and the endless spilling of blood and shattering of limbs in Vietnam. From daily television they were exposed to information and sensations experienced by no previous generation. The four-year-old child who watches a television program about blue babies may be able to handle that; but can she manage a program in which a middle-aged mother suddenly decides to leave her husband and four-year-old child? What happens to an eleven-year-old repeatedly exposed to television soap operas which stress extramarital affairs? How does the thirteen-year-old take in the massacre at My Lai? It is just possible that their systems, at least some of them, suffer from awareness-overload.

CHOICE-OVERLOAD

The young may be depressed by choice-overload too. Teenagers in middle-class America are confronted with an astounding array of choices. The choices that accompany affluence—choosing between handbags, dresses and movies—account for relatively little pressure on teenagers. The choices that hurt have to do with friends, sex, drugs, parents and school. The old rules governing choices in such matters—and drugs were not an issue in any previous generation—are more tenuous than ever. For many of the young they don't even exist. Since the choices are their own, they soliloquize and argue constantly within themselves. Drugs present a constant dilemma.

"Should I try speed again?"

"Why not?"

"Because I don't want to become addicted."

"Did you become addicted to pot?"

"No, but speed is different."

"How is it different?"

"It's even better; it makes you feel really good."

"If it makes you feel good, what is so bad?"

"I might try something else."

"That's not logical; how does that follow?"

"That's what I said when I tried pot."

"Well, you liked pot."

"Yes, but speed kills."

"Not if you just have it once in a while."

"Besides, they might find out."

"Who?"

"Mom and Dad."

"What if they do?"

"I don't want to hurt them."

"That's their problem. We don't stop them from trying speed."

"What about the police?"

"What about them?"

"I might get caught."

"Only if you're careless."

Choices concerning friends and sex are more complicated than ever.

"Should I go with him?"

"Why not?"

"He's Sally's boyfriend."

"So what?"

"Well, I'm loyal to her."

"How about your own feelings?"

"My own feelings?"

"Aren't you loyal to them?"

"But I don't want to hurt Sally."

"You'll hurt her more and yourself if you're dishonest."

"What about sex?"

"What about it?"

"He'll want to go to bed."

"So what?"

"I don't know if I want to."

"How will you ever know if you don't try?"

"But will it ever be the same between him, Sally and me?"

"Nothing is ever the same."

These are the choices that make the adult charge that adolescents have too much too soon more than just a mindless criticism. Choices are burdensome. Should a sixteen-year-old be expected to make a decision between an abortion and getting married? Even if youth culture sanctions abortion, she still may be deeply frightened. Parents often seem unable to help. If parents don't know what they are talking about—as is often the case with drugs—or seem unsuccessful in their personal relations— as is often the case in marriage—how can one accept their answers or tentative advice?

SCHOOLS ARE PART OF THE PROBLEM

Schools are the place where answers are organized and it is in schools that the young spend a great deal of their time. Since schools purport to be authoritative, even when parents do not, it is against schools that adolescents direct much of their hostility. The explanation for increasing depression in and anger against schools is not hard to find. As studies show, today's high-school and early-college students are about a year more mature sexually than their parents at the same age (the onset of puberty keeps coming earlier) and approximately one grade level ahead of where their parents were at the same age. Yet, the young remain in school approximately five years longer, thus deferring adult responsibility for half a decade more. As a consequence, soliliquies like this one are not unusual:

"Why should I study?"
"To get through school."
"Why get through school?"
"To get to another school."
"What's the point?"
"To make money."
"Why make money?"
"To buy things."
"That's no reason."
"Well, I want an interesting job."
"Why should you?"
"Because life is dull without one."
"But school is duller than anything."

Complaints against the schools by many of the young bear little resemblance to old-fashioned griping about this or that teacher or principal. Many are saying that the schools are prisons, where they feel trapped or suffocated. Despite the defeat of bond issues, more money is spent on education than ever before, particularly in the suburbs. New buildings, fancy equipment, teachers with higher degrees are the order of the day. Yet the schools, by failing to keep pace with the vast changes that have taken place in the total experience of the young, not only fail to relieve the depression of many of them but actually contribute to it.

One does not have to agree with the mindless assumption that the young know what is best for their own education to appreciate how inappropriate is much of the education they receive. Nor does one have to accept the assertion that the necessarily best way to learn is through direct personal experience to realize that the lock-step, print-based method of education pervasive in the schools is at sharp variance with the more immediate, direct, sensory, experiential learning that takes place outside.

〈At the very time that adolescents are awakening to the excitement, contradictions, agonies and possibilities of human behavior, the study of human behavior in the secondary schools remains largely didactic, sterile and banal. At the moment in history when young people have become aware of human problems through visual awareness, the schools make practically no use of television as a basis for social studies〉 It is exactly because the study of human behavior is in its early stages—not easily codified and passed on through textbooks—that schools have been so lethargic in exploiting its possibilities. But it is precisely for that reason that the study of human behavior can be most engaging—a subject to which we will return in the last chapter.

If schools were educationally exciting, there would be less call for student power. What is needed more than a student-centered curriculum is a significance-centered curriculum. Those educational experiments which purport to have the students define significance have not been notably successful in either liberating them from depression or leading them toward intellectual achievement. Whereas traditional schools deny students the self-esteem which comes from applying one's experience and engaging in work, so-called free schools and most new experimental schools and colleges have failed to provide the structure which the young invariably require to develop self-confidence. But it is not structureless education for which the students cry, although it may seem so to them at times, but a structure which is appropriate to their needs. Where authority is imaginative, sensitive, responsible (not just acquiescent), the results seem much better than when there is little or no authority at all. Where schools are dull and authority is imposed irrationally to keep the pressure on the young, adolescents often mistake the issue of substance for form. They cry for student control because they mistakenly see no other way to get what they want—an education for living.

REJECTING THE EFFICIENCY ETHIC

The depression and unrest of the young have been particularly noticeable among the upper-middle-class seg-
ment of that generation which came to consciousness in
the 1960's. A minority among them see themselves as
forerunners of a cultural revolution in America, a revolution of values. The attitudes of the majority of the twenty-
three million young men and women of college age
(eighteen to twenty-four) are not much different from
those of their parents' generation, according to studies
made since 1969. There have been differences with their
parents over the length of their hair, and more important,
the war in Vietnam, but a majority still accept the culture's emphasis on achievement through productivity and
work. They value political stability, economic competition and hard work. Even among the middle-class young
there is a growing skepticism about the so-called counter-
culture. Among the lower-middle-class young there is considerable hostility to the self-styled upper-middle-class
radicals who decry the establishment (the high-schoolers
fight each other in alleys and school halls), and for them
and the children of the poor there is little of the Holden
Caulfield sense of near-total psychological isolation.
Lower-middle-class adolescents do not worry as much
about self-discovery as making it; the children of the poor
are likely to be more concerned with sheer survival and
their identity as poor whites, Blacks, Chicanos, Puerto
Ricans or Indians than with intra-psychic salvation.

If one looks at the results of detailed surveys on the
young and the spate of books written in recent years by

youth issues

youthful spokesmen for cultural revolution, certain dominant themes appear. The major criticism by the radicals is
that the emphasis on productivity in American life has
been dehumanizing. They argue that productivity-centered values, such as work, planning, organization, efficiency, savings and investment, often lead to mechanical
and sometimes exploitative human relationships. The
cultural revolutionaries, except for a tiny faction, are not
politically radical. At what may have been the height of
political agitation in 1969, a comprehensive *Fortune*
magazine survey showed that only 20 percent of the self-
styled revolutionaries in college admired Stokely Car-
michael and Che Guevara compared with 65 percent and
56 percent for Senators Eugene McCarthy and Edward
Kennedy, respectively.

Yet it seems clear that Vietnam has been the quintes-
sence of what is wrong in America from the point of view
of the radical young. (Sixty-seven percent of the radical
college youth in the *Fortune* survey felt that draft resistance was justified under any circumstances.) The war
encapsuled all of the values associated with productivity:
purpose, planning, efficiency, numbers, impersonality,
dehumanization, lovelessness. The two men charged with
explaining the war, Presidents Lyndon Johnson and Richard Nixon, could hardly have been less convincing, partly
because of the internal contradictions in the substance of
their argument. Johnson and Nixon, insisting on the need
to spend two billion dollars a month to kill in Vietnam
while talking about peace, appeared to be dishonest men.
While speaking of peace, the Presidents and their spokes-

V. war

men seemed ever concerned with kill-ratios, public opinion polls and numbers generally. In addition, the young, preoccupied with matters of style, were critical of the establishment style which Johnson and Nixon seemed to typify. Style is a slippery concept, difficult to define. Yet there were certain adjectives applied consistently to both Presidents by youthful critics—"controlled," "uptight," "manipulative" and "phony"—indicating their preoccupation with style rather than content. Oversimplified and harsh as these judgments may seem, youthful cultural radicals have seen in Johnson and Nixon the end products of a society which values success through competition and cares about productivity and quantity as opposed to love and quality. The argument of the radical critics may seem exaggerated, but consider for a moment that some young people are using different standards for judging themselves and others than those employed in previous generations. If that is true, then we are witnessing what may be the beginning of a revolution against the dominant values of the culture. Revolution is a terribly complex subject—cultural revolution even more than the political—but perhaps a greatly oversimplified model of vast changes in values in the past can help explain what is happening now.

In traditional, preindustrial societies, where roles, functions and statuses are clearly defined, individuals value themselves and others in terms of how they are able to answer the question, How do we fit in? The issue is whether one is what one is supposed to be and whether one does what one is supposed to do. Individuals look upon themselves as units of integration. How does one fit into the family, clan, village, nature, cosmos? That is what matters. This is not a question of getting along with a group of one's peers or being accepted in a new situation. It is a lifelong issue. What is important is knowing one's place in time, space, work and relationships.

As men and women move from traditional societies toward industrialization, they begin to think less of themselves and others as units of integration and more as units of productivity. The critical question becomes, How effective am I (or is he or she)? Productivity rather than group harmony and survival becomes the goal. Control, purposefulness and the postponing of immediate pleasure in order to produce are important. Once relationships become more competitive, men become more wary of each other. When relationships become more contractual (organized for the purpose of accomplishing a task), they also become more temporary and less dependable. If individuals become more socially mobile (downward as well as upward), they will be more anxious in relationships (especially in a democracy, since popularity becomes a manifestation as well as a source of success). When productivity is linked to personal achievement, as opposed to group achievement, as in the Japanese corporate enterprise or a Jewish family, a kind of psychological isolation ensues that is unknown in traditional societies. The result is that men and women, desperately needing and wanting dependable love, find it more difficult to share in families than in traditional societies. These are the consequences for human relationships, say some of the radical young, when individuals think and feel in terms of productivity. Life becomes programmed. Groups and individuals become tracked. Efficiency becomes the dominant principle for organizing life. Other aspects of man's nature are neglected or subverted.

The analysis is obviously one-sided. The negative aspects of productivity-centered values are stressed; the benefits are not even acknowledged. The emphasis on productivity has meant that human beings are healthier, eat better, live longer and have richly expanded their knowledge. It is easy to see why parents and grandparents who have worked hard to see their offspring eat at a full table and receive an Ivy League education are dismayed at the increasingly frequent youthful reaction of "So what?" We should remember that the proportion who exclaim "So what?" is still a minority of the college population, but the sudden rejection of the values centered around productivity by so many of the young must be accounted for.

EXPRESSION AS EXPERIENCE

The generation which came to consciousness in the 1960's is different from any generation which preceded it. It is the first generation to be so acutely aware of its loneliness and depression as a group. It is the first generation to write books and songs, publish newspapers and make movies for large-scale consumption which attack the efficiency values of the culture.

But there are thousands among those who grew up in the 1960's who are not depressed and who do not verbally attack the values of productivity but whose very lives indicate the rejection of those values. They live quietly on rural communes, organize macrobiotic food stores and restaurants, practice Yoga, join Back-to-Jesus movements, help Ralph Nadar, or enlist in the Peace Corps or VISTA. They share with those who are more depressed or angry a searching for new values, an attitude against organization, planning and efficiency, although they do not make a big thing of their rejection of the older productivity values. That their basic stance is so alike is not surprising, since they are all children of the 1960's, all part of a generation reared under fundamentally new forces.

Children of Psychology

The first of these new forces was psychology. This was the first self-consciously psychological generation raised by self-consciously psychological parents. Whatever the thrust of Freud's writing may have been to more sophisticated students of human behavior, the popular impact has been a widespread and growing awareness of the subconscious. While Freud believed that repression had its place in turning children into civilized adults, the popular interpretation of Freud's emphasis on the subconscious was that it ought to be expressed. American middle-class parents in the late forties, fifties and early sixties, spurred by the vague knowledge that self-expression is healthy, moved rapidly, as we have seen, toward more permissive child-rearing practices. The watchword for the more permissive was: Don't frustrate the child; let him express himself.

A second consequence of the dissemination of psychological knowledge about the subconscious was to encourage an increasing awareness of the distinction between appearances and reality. Society, by and large, was organized for appearances. The generation that came to consciousness in the sixties was the first to find that truism despicable. People, it was seen, lived in an inner self and an outer self. Only the former was real. Many young people do armchair psychoanalysis on their principals, teachers and parents. If you are over forty, it is highly unlikely that you did the same to Herbert Hoover, Franklin Roosevelt or your teachers and parents. Thus, a generation of upper-middle-class children grew up with a new psychological orientation which seemed to tell them that there was something like inner experience and outer experience, and that outer experience really wasn't experience at all but a kind of role-playing guided by the values of productivity—therefore, those values were bad. Self-expression—being true to one's feelings in expression—was good.

Children of Affluence

One way to express oneself is by making choices. The discussion earlier of choice-overload indicated how psychologically troubling choices about relationships or drugs can be. Other kinds of choices proliferated for the middle-class young in the 1960's which are more directly attributable to the surging affluence of that decade. If psychological knowledge made new experience via self-expression desirable, affluence made many new experiences possible. Some of those experiences undoubtedly bring sheer pleasure, which reinforces the desire for experience for its own sake as opposed to the old notion of experience in order to get ahead (or even to learn). Affluence leads to consumption, which leads to new experience, including the values of other cultures and a questioning of established values. (In recent summers more than seven hundred thousand Americans under thirty traveled to other lands.) Consumption is a form of self-expression; it and other aspects of self-expression become a new way of defining experience as opposed to saving, working and other values associated with getting ahead.

It may seem ironic that the affluent young have been the first to denounce on such a large scale materialism and the values which produced it, but it is only after one is rich that it is possible to discover the poverty of wealth. It is foolish to romanticize the richness of poverty, since pain, disease and empty bellies never felt good, but at least it is clear that in a society which has attained great wealth, emotional and spiritual health does not necessarily follow.

Children of Television
Freud, affluence and technology are the things that made growing up in America in the 1960's so different from what it was for previous generations, and in no other phenomenon did these three come together with as much

power as through television. Historians of the future may decide that the most significant force in the lives of the young in the 1960's was the development and spread of television. In 1945 there were only six television stations in the nation; twenty years later there were 586 and 92 percent of American households had one or more television sets. By 1970 it was estimated that the average American seventeen-year-old had already watched 18,000 hours of television, or slightly more than two years of his life. Of course, the majority among the young who hold traditional values centered on productivity have watched as much television as the culture critics; but they probably respond to television differently. For the more radical among the young the medium is much more the message than for others. They produce and enjoy psychedelic light shows at home and at coffeehouses. They also make movies to interpret their way of looking at the world, but perhaps what is most important about their efforts in photography as well as their consumption of television is that they stimulate sensory awareness and vitiate the credibility of print as a form of communication.

Because visual experiences are powerful and seem complete, many of the young have become mistrustful of other kinds of communication. They have also learned to distrust the words of political leaders whose utterances seem contradicted by the images seen on TV. An official explanation on Vietnam, whether read in the newspapers or viewed on TV, can be destroyed by the pictures one sees through the tube. The Vietnam war was brought to the playrooms of young, affluent Americans, who learned to judge for themselves, however superficially, whether or not their President was telling the truth. Print could not do that for the majority of previous generations. Only television can communicate so quickly and powerfully to large numbers of citizens.

GROPING FOR NEW VALUES

For a substantial minority of the young who grew up in the 1960's, the popularization of Freud, the spread of affluence and the impact of television combined to undermine the values connected with productivity and to encourage new ways of evaluating human life. Whereas pre-industrial man thought of himself as a unit of integration and industrial man as a unit of productivity, self-proclaimed cultural revolutionaries tend to value experience through expression and consumption. The key questions become: Am I open to experience? Do I feel it? Do I express it (not necessarily in words)? Always, the "I" is at the center of concern. The search for experience, to understand and express oneself, seems endless, and to many of their critics, the present high school and college generation seems as though it must be the most narcissistic in history. To some of these, the young appear to be forever peering into a vacuum with a microscope. From the point of view of the young, they are searching for new values based on personal experience to replace the rejected values passed on by previous generations. In defense of what often seems to others like orgiastic introspection, the young would reply that they are the first generation to try to get in touch with their own deep feelings, the first to search for an authentic self. The young admit that they are self-centered. In the *Fortune* survey, 43 percent of the "radicals" saw themselves as more self-centered than their parents compared with 17 percent who thought their parents were more self-centered. They have accepted the ideology of personal independence no less than their parents, and have given it even stronger emphasis. When asked to define success in a way that reflected their own personal values, 73 percent of the college "radicals" said, "Doing your own thing," while only a little more than a third checked "Being a respected leader in the community." (Respondents were permitted to check more than one item from several on a list.)

Yet these same students see themselves as much more interested in other people, concerned with what is happening to the country, open to the world and more tolerant of other people's values than their parents. Apparent paradoxes abound. While acknowledging that they are more self-centered, they also claim to be more open to and interested in others. It is not surprising that there is in some young men and women an intolerance of those who disagree with them which seems to wipe out their assertion of openness. If the young are so certain of being more virtuous than their parents, it is not likely that they are going to be more tolerant of those who disagree with them. In their defense against the charge of intolerance, they accuse their parents of phony tolerance (which it often may be) that veils prejudice and disagreement while the young and oppressed minorities are kept in their places. "Why be tolerant," a radical might ask, "of a system which dehumanizes human beings?" The central paradox, they would assert, is easy to resolve. Self-centeredness which is based on being true to one's experience means being put together in a wholesome, healthy way. And that, it would be argued, is a precondition to being genuinely in touch with and concerned about others. Thus, the searing intolerance which one finds so often among the most radical culture critics is defended in the name of human development and called by the name of honesty.

THE AUTHENTIC SELF?

The supreme value of the new culture appears to be the discovery and expression of the authentic self, a process (not a product) which can be conducted in many ways. It is undertaken through drugs, basic encounter groups, relationships, art, music or religious mysticism. Rarely is it seen as having anything to do with work except on communal farms or through handiwork such as jewelry-making or leatherwork, or in cooking and carpentry. Least of all can it take place in school, where society presents organized answers to questions rarely raised by the young themselves. While the pursuit of the authentic self is often agonizing, many young people report a heightened awareness of self as a result of experience with drugs, encounter groups or special diets. A fundamental question cuts through the rhetoric about self-discovery. To what extent is the taking of marijuana, for example, an attempt to discover and express oneself as opposed to an effort to escape aspects of oneself or obligations to others which are felt as terrible burdens? Of course, the same question can be asked of alcohol users of any age. Alcohol, marijuana, encounter-group sessions, fasting, prayer and other activities often bring poignant moments of self-discovery as well as relief from mental anguish and physical discomfort. Soaring highs, when they do occur, may at the same moment be both discovery and escape. One thing is certain: from such highs students and others must come down. The growing use of drugs on the college and high school campuses of America may bring more highs, but widespread depression remains a fact of life among the young.

Undoubtedly contributing to the depression of many of the cultural revolutionaries is the fact that their own definition of new values is still quite murky. It is extremely difficult to attempt to create a counterculture based on new values when those values are only dimly understood. It is particularly trying when one's life is governed to a large extent by institutions based on the old productivity values which have been repudiated. One of those values most scorned is power. Cultural revolutionaries do not know how to deal with it and are not sure they want to. They are not interested in the planning, organization, efficiency and salesmanship which make for success in politics. They are into other things. Some are into smashing the system altogether, but a vast majority simply want a new one without knowing how to get there or even where there is. It took many generations following the industrial revolution to replace the values of a traditional peasant society with those of a modern, productive one (and many traditional societies are now going through the agony of transition), and even longer before new institutions such as political parties, corporations and trade unions emerged. Some of the young will answer that new institutions will come from their fidelity to the values which grow out of being real. But the search for the authentic self is endless and often seems characterized by confusion, irresolution and even joylessness.

FLEEING FROM AND FIGHTING DEPRESSION

What does all this have to do with independence and equality in families? My own view is that the depression of so many of the middle-class young is exacerbated by the American preoccupation with independence and equality. Being counted on and being responsible for and obligated to others in the family cause them discomfort. They seek a sense of belonging with strangers or peers in relationships which, no matter how intense, are tenuous, and when broken, leave a flat, empty, aching feeling of aloneness. What does one do with depression? Clinical studies show that the extremely depressed either withdraw or get angry.

While the growing use of marijuana undoubtedly is an expression of the desire for new experience and is perhaps connected to a larger search for new values to replace fallen ones, pot and other drugs are for many of the young —as drugs are for people everywhere in the world—a way of escaping pain and misery. This is not to say that young men and women do not use pot widely for social reasons and simple pleasure. It is to assert what the young know so well themselves. Drugs, including marijuana, are often used by young people to withdraw from depression and as a way of separating themselves from their families.

The same motivation to relieve depression, although less obvious, sometimes applies to sexual relationships. Like drugs, sex can be a way both of relieving depression and of causing it. When sex fails to live up to expectations, the reaction for some young people—not unlike their elders—is to turn to it compulsively as a way of withdrawing further from the personal and social problems which inundate them. Of course, in many ways sex is viewed differently from drugs by the young. For one thing, although they have sexual problems as do their elders, their general attitude toward sex is that it is wholesome and not harmful in any way. Of course, there is strong pressure on many girls to conform to an open sex ethic which is disturbing to some of them. But for the most part, the young seem to have more healthy attitudes and sex lives in college than did their parents, and for many it is a major source of pleasure. As with drugs, the motivation and the results are mixed.

Sex and drugs can provide ways of withdrawing to relieve depression. Anger also can provide relief. The angry young seem to be more political than the cultural radicals who withdraw. From the point of view of society, anger can be an important instrument of social and political change. But when anger is largely the consequence of deep depression, the causes of which are not even understood, it is likely to be misdirected and ineffective.

So ingrained has anger become for some of the young, that they have made it into a life style. Indeed, some young Americans appear to have replaced old-fashioned ritual politeness with ritual anger. Yet they do not recognize their outbursts of hostility as rituals. To the contrary, getting angry is given—and often taken—as a sign of one's authenticity. The old phoniness against which Holden Caulfield complained may have been replaced by a new one. Although there is much genuine anger among the young, it is difficult to know what each expression of anger means. The student who interrupts his professor in the large lecture hall with screams of "Bullshit" may be saying one or more of several things:

—"Professor, you are wrong."
—"Look, everybody, how I defy a professor and show how independent and honest I am."
—"I'll tell the world how much it stinks—the professor, this school, and everyone who is trying to run my life."

Of these statements the first is least likely to be what the student really means. The student who yells "Bullshit" in such a situation probably is not interested in arguing about the facts or the logic of the professor's statement. What probably matters most is that he wants recognition as a person. His anger may be more or less ritualistic, but it comes from a deep sense of alienation from a society which he feels—however confusedly—oppresses him.

In my view, he is—no less than his parents—the victim

of an ideal which he understands least of all, the ideal of the independent, self-sufficient self. It is striking that neither the cultural revolutionaries nor the political radicals have attacked the sacred cow of personal independence. They have not only made it their own; they act as though they invented it. True to their Jeffersonian inheritance, the angry organizers of the Students for Democratic Action in 1962 issued a manifesto (fifty-two single-spaced pages) which celebrated personal independence. Sharply criticizing society, they called for a "democracy of individual participation, governed by two central aims: that the individual share in those social decisions that determine the quality and direction of his life; [and] that society be organized to encourage independence in men . . ." It was a pronouncement, at least that particular portion of it, to which Andrew Jackson, Theodore Roosevelt, Herbert Hoover and Barry Goldwater would have subscribed enthusiastically. Whereas Goldwater would see the threat to individual independence as coming from big government, SDS and other radical activists see a conspiracy among big government, business and the military (some would include the universities, of course) to suppress the individual.

While the ideology of many of the political radicals owes more to Jefferson than to Marx, the stance of the cultural revolutionaries clearly is Emerson's. Who knows what kind of parent Emerson would be today? Would he hold fast to the parochial American view that valuable learning comes only through direct personal experience? How would he apply that idea to the adolescent son who seeks personal salvation through LSD? The questions may seem foolish, since they can be answered only by guesswork. But there is a relationship between Emerson and Jimi Hendrix, the drug-racked, alienated Black rock singer and guitarist whose songs on self-reliance were applauded by hundreds of thousands of young Americans in the late 1960's and early 1970's, even after he died from an overdose of drugs. When Hendrix sang his popular "If Six Was Nine," he reckoned that if six turned out to be nine, if the sun refused to shine or if the mountains fell in the sea, it wouldn't matter to him because "Got my own life to live through/and I ain't goin' to copy you." Hendrix concluded that song with a plea to "let me live my life the way I want to," an updating of Emerson for contemporary adolescents.

An Emersonian interpretation of Hendrix's death might hold that he was a victim of social forces which did not let him be free to be the individual he wanted to be. Another view—central to this book—is that Hendrix may have been victimized by the cult of individualism itself, which not only cuts Americans off from their ancestors and blocks their links to the future but which also makes it so difficult for them to give and receive dependable love.

DEPENDENCY IS A DIRTY WORD
FOR THE YOUNG AND THE OLD

It seems that many of the young have replaced an older form of dependency on parents and families with a new one on psychiatrists, group-therapy sessions, fleeting relationships and drugs in their frantic search to "live my life the way I want to." Having been taught that dependency is a dirty word, many seem to want love without obligation, affection without responsibility. They turn from these terms—obligation and responsibility—because the words seem tied to an older system of family dependence which keeps people from being true to their feelings. But there is no escape for human beings from dependency, despite American mythology to the contrary. In the kingdom of the young, the old continue to mythologize about childhood and youth. To be young, many imagine, is to have a Tom Sawyer-like time of true independence, when illnesses are slight and responsibilities nonexistent.

Long before they reach sixty or even fifty, Americans become apprehensive about aging. Women of that age often speak of themselves as "girls" or sometimes even "dolls"; men of that age, panicked at the prospect of growing older, sometimes grab at a new vision of youthfulness which used to be called "a second childhood." The clutching at youthfulness occurs in no other society because nowhere else have the old been so stripped of prestige, power and function. And nowhere else are they so separated from their families!

In traditional societies the old have more prestige than the young because they know more and are counted on to make valuable contributions to society until their death. They have more power because their authority over their children and grandchildren continues. They function as vital parts of an ongoing society, as priests, chieftains, leaders, warriors, mothers-in-law, grandmothers, aunts and in other valued roles. They receive more love because it is the responsibility of the family to take care of them even when they are sick and infirm.

In the United States the old must often come to terms courageously and with as much dignity as they can muster with creaking joints, pains, bad digestion and failing mental facilities without the close support of children and grandchildren who are busy and productive. What makes the problem more serious now than in previous times is that while the very old are more numerous, a much smaller proportion of them are gainfully employed. Those over sixty-five make up one-tenth of the population in the United States compared with only 4 percent in 1900. Now less than 25 percent of them are employed full time, mainly because of enforced retirement policies, compared with about 67 percent at the turn of the century. The group is large, the problems larger. Yet, in all of the media, probably not one-hundredth of the attention is given to the aged and their problems as is given to youth.

It was not long ago in the United States that most families strongly felt their responsibility to take personal care of the very old. But in recent years the American response to the growing population of the old has been to place them in institutions or to encourage them to live by themselves. In the last fifteen years, the nursing-home business has multiplied more than ten times in dollar value. In the decade of the sixties nearly half a million new beds in nursing homes for the elderly were created; yet the demand is so strong that a great majority of nursing homes—as inferior as they may be—are at least 80 percent full a year after they open. The percentage of the aged living in institutions is still slight—less than 10 percent in 1970—but it is growing. More than a fifth of the men over sixty-five and one-third of the women over sixty-five live alone. But even those who live with families often lead lonely lives.

The plight of the very old is widely talked about in the United States, but the heart of the matter is little understood. No commission on the aged or Medicare program gets at the root of the problem. Having been raised on and having preached the ideal of independence, the old are in no position to turn from it when they most need help. They have been convinced that there is shame in being dependent. A study by one of my students of articles in popular women's and other magazines over the past decade dealing with the question of the elderly and their care shows that American writers are fairly consistent in their treatment of the question. While understanding that the elderly feel discarded and useless because society makes them feel that way, they conclude invariably that what grandma and grandpa need is more independence. The warning to children is clear: Don't overprotect them lest they become dependent. Perhaps the problem is that they really are dependent, not just that they feel it. Of course, surveys show that a majority of the old prefer to live alone. What else can they say? The culture has told them that the best thing they can do is to stay out of the way of their children and grandchildren. But in addition to the pain we have caused the aged by making them feel useless, Americans have deprived their young by cutting them off from the old.

When the Netsilik Eskimos take the long winter journey to hunt seals, the aged are sometimes left behind to die. But the Netsilik have few choices if they want to survive as a family unit. There is simply not enough food to go around. That is not the situation of Americans. Surely they can be more inventive in bringing grandparents back into the lives of their grandchildren or, at the very least, the grandchildren of others. Even when they are physically separated from their own families, more frequent visiting should be possible than usually takes place. It is the attitude which is crucial. Grandparents are afraid to take the initiative because grandchildren often are so uninterested. Grandchildren are uninterested because they have been taught that what is old-fashioned in America is obsolescent. Yet the stories of their grandparents are the fascinating stuff of history, of life itself. There are dozens of small programs in the country now attempting to break the pattern of the segregation of the old from the young, but they are not likely to get very far until Americans see the problem for what it really is.

It is no accident that the subject of aging has received special treatment from the best American writers of dramatic tragedy. The crisis for men usually comes some time around fifty-five, as in the case of Willy Loman in Arthur Miller's *Death of a Salesman*. It is a crisis described poignantly by psychiatrist Erik Erikson, who sees it as one of integrity versus stagnation. Miller's salesman, like so many other men, can face the future with confidence only if he has some sense of having succeeded on his own in the past. Tennessee Williams' play *Sweet Bird of Youth* revolves around an aging actress who tries to avoid the pains of aging through sex, drugs and liquor. In both plays the dramatist depicts the loss of dignity and the sense of uselessness that frequently plague the aging in America. Edward Albee concentrates on the very old in *Sandbox* and *The American Dream*. In the first, the plot brings eighty-six-year-old grandma to a beach with mommy and daddy, who place her in a sandbox to await her death. In the second, mommy and daddy permit grandma to live with them but under the constant threat of sending her away if she is "not good." Grandma's dependency is total.

While sensitive dramatists reveal the plight of the very old, the subject is overlooked in popular movies, literature and television precisely because the culture discards the old. So, in looking at the old and the young, we come full circle. The young are particularly precocious; the old feel particularly useless. The young assert the authority they cannot possibly assume; the very old, totally bereft of authority, cling to the fiction of independence while being kept alive by modern medicine, checks from Social Security and the fear of death. As long as they, their doctors and especially their children worship the sacred cow of independence, they will feel guilty when they desire help from their sons and daughters.

Is it not possible that the depression of the very old is related to that of adolescents? Should they both—should we all—look the sacred cow right in the eye?

III On Being Female in America

Seen from the perspective of outsiders, American women are pampered, spoiled, assertive, powerful and remarkably independent. On this point the comments of visitors from Asia, Europe, Africa and South America have been consistent from the beginning of the eighteenth century to the present. The United States of America, they have maintained, is a woman's paradise.

Yet American women have from the earliest days of the republic protested more loudly and vigorously than any other group of females against their subordination by males. There is no paradox in this revolt in paradise. American women usually have been freer than women elsewhere (except for the very rich in some eras and places in Europe and Asia); but spurred by the ideals of independence and equality, they have been more conscious of inequities that exist between the sexes in their own society.

Today the movement for the liberation of women from male domination is gaining in many countries, but nowhere is it so strong as in America. Much confusion arises in discussion about the liberation of women because of a failure to distinguish between two related but different arguments: first, women are discriminated against in employment and politics; second, women are subjugated in their roles as wives and mothers. The first finds many sympathizers—men and women who will agree quickly that the sexes should be paid equally for equal work and that they should have genuinely equal opportunities in employment and politics. Confusion is caused by the contention that the oppression of women in society as a whole stems from their exploitation as wives and mothers. On this point, there is widespread resistance.

The reason is not hard to find. Whether a woman is paid fairly is a matter of economics and politics. Whether a woman becomes a wife or mother—and what those roles mean—have to do with biology as well as culture. To what extent the roles usually played by wives, mothers and fathers are modifiable depends on much more knowledge of the biological basis of male–female differences and inequalities than is available. But almost everyone in America now agrees that male domination of females has often meant irrational oppression and exploitation of them.

RATIONALIZATION FOR MALE DOMINANCE

Long after its origin, men justified patriarchy with the creation of magnificent myths: the intellectual inferiority of females; their uncleanness and sinfulness; their demonic sexuality and, contradictorily, their lack of sexuality. Such myths sanctioned the abuse of women. For example, the Koran expressly grants the right to husbands to beat recalcitrant wives—a practice also widely condoned in Christendom throughout most of its history.

Each of the major forces in the shaping of Western civilization—Hebraic, Roman, Greek and Christian—has contributed to the subordination of women. The ancient Hebrews believed that husbands and fathers must be given power to command so that the entire family could fulfill God's law. The Jews made stringent rules which checked the abuse of male power and never justified patriarchy in terms of either female inferiority or sinfulness, but as in many cultures, they believed women were unclean during menstruation and made them perform a ceremony of ritual purification. The Romans and Greeks continually emphasized the inferiority of the female intellect. Before Aristotle, it was widely believed among the Greeks that the female had no active role in

male myths

conception, that the child developed from the coagulation of the seminal fluid of the man when deposited in the womb of the woman; the only function of the female was to serve as an incubator. If the woman contributes nothing of her essential self to the making of the child and is just the soil which nourishes the seed, she is a lesser partner in perpetuating life from generation to generation. It is impossible to know how important this misconception was in justifying male dominance, but it continued in the West after this myth was discarded mainly because of the Christian interpretation of the sinfulness of woman and her demonic sexuality. The works of saints—Paul, Jerome, Augustine, Ambrose and Thomas—contributed to the myth of female evil.* Ambrose pointed out that "Adam was deceived by Eve, not Eve by Adam . . . it is right that he whom the woman induced to sin should assume the role of guide lest he fall again through feminine instability." "The Devil's gateway" was an early Christian label for women. The Church writers of the Middle Ages believed that women were insatiably lustful—the incarnation of the vice of unchastity. Paradoxically, the cult of the Virgin, which was flourishing in the twelfth century, laid the basis for the contrary view of females as having a higher morality than males because they were less sexual.

It was that view which began to prevail widely in the West in the nineteenth century despite the fact that the

---

* Hindus and Buddhists also developed such myths. The Brahmins used to say, "Educate a woman and you put a knife into the hands of a monkey." Some Buddhist temples were forbidden to women because of the fear of contamination.

robust sexuality of females had been written and sung about, mostly among the lower classes, for centuries. The relatively new myth of superior male sexuality was apparently confirmed in the behavior of animals. It seemed as though males were sexually aggressive and females passive. (We now know that female chimps, gorillas and orangutans in heat initiate sex.) Female animals were limited to definite periods of estrus within which they made themselves available sexually. As for human females, menstruation and long periods of responsibility for carrying and nursing infants *presumably* inhibited their desire and capacity for sexual intercourse. Females were passive and that was the way they should be. By the late nineteenth century that ideal was so strongly entrenched that the surgeon general of the U.S. Army proclaimed in 1864 that decent women experienced absolutely no pleasure in sex. When the English physician Havelock Ellis demanded sexual equality for women he was resoundingly denounced. Despite the sexual freedom of the twenties, when lipsticks, rumble seats and short skirts became commonplace, women were still thought to be relatively passive sexually. Probably millions of men and women assumed that females were actually incapable of achieving orgasms.

THE REDISCOVERY OF EVE

By the middle of the twentieth century, new knowledge brought forth new attitudes. It was discovered that in some cultures women commonly initiated sex (this is true among the Hopi, Trobrianders, Kwamis, Maoris,

Dahomeans, and in Bali and elsewhere). But the impact of anthropological investigations was slight compared with the findings of Alfred Kinsey. Superficially, his studies seemed to confirm the stronger sexuality of males. For example, while 68 percent of college-educated men had experienced intercourse before marriage, only 50 percent of college-educated women had done so. More significantly, although almost 100 percent of the males had had an orgasm by the age of seventeen, only 30 percent of the females had experienced orgasm before marriage. Ten percent of the women interviewed had apparently never experienced sexual climax, and maximum orgasmic response in the female was not reached until the age of thirty-five. But other information revealed by Kinsey made it clear that compared with other primates, human females are unusually sexual, even though their genital sexual activity may develop more slowly than in men. According to Kinsey and others, only the human female—no other female animal—commonly experiences orgasm in intercourse.* While most other females are ready for sex only at times of fertility (making nature's procreative purpose clear), the human female seems to be quite desirous of sex just before and after her period when she is least fertile, indicating that in addition to procreation, nature had sexual pleasure in mind for her. The Kinsey study showed a fantastic range of sexual experience among women—much greater than that for men.

---

* After studying baboons for many years Irven DeVore, the leading baboon ethologist, states that the female in intercourse definitely acts as if she is having an orgasm.

Some women reported having many orgasms within a few moments (the multiple orgasm). Young women told the Kinsey interviewers of experiencing fifty orgasms in a single month. Later, Masters and Johnson would report that they observed women achieve fifty or more orgasms in an hour through clitoral-area stimulation. The studies of Kinsey not only helped to legitimize sex for women but promoted it. With the widespread use of effective birth-control methods, particularly the pill in the 1960's, new possibilities emerged for the expression of female sexuality. The age-old fear of pregnancy was sharply reduced for the first time, encouraging a kind of sexual freedom previously known only to men. Quick to recognize the significance of the change, advertisers, publishers and movie-makers blatantly portrayed female sexuality in their products. Men appeared to be increasingly on the defensive sexually. Women, becoming more aware of their sexuality, demanded satisfaction from their men. In the past, the problems of impotence and premature ejaculation undoubtedly were widespread, but they were not talked or written about. In marriages where Victorian morality prevailed, they might not even have mattered, since women were not expected to enjoy sex. Now, with men feeling the pressure to perform effectively as never before, those problems are not only talked about, they have become more serious.

THE DOUBLE STANDARD UNDER ATTACK

The double standard, while always less important in America than in Europe, came under sharp attack in the

1960's. For centuries the double standard in Europe had been justified by two main assumptions: the pressing sexual needs of males and the importance of female chastity. It was widely thought, particularly in Catholic-Latin countries, that males needed frequent sex to relieve constant physical tension and to demonstrate their masculinity in competition with others (undoubtedly, the male terror at being made a cuckold has deep roots in the prehistory of the species when males competed for the use and possession of females). It was also assumed that the absence of female chastity before marriage might signify a potentiality for looseness after marriage which would lead to a confusion of progeny and a diffusion of property. That is why a maid who lost her virginity was described in the sixteenth century in England as "unthrifty," and it was believed, as one English poet wrote, that "wives lose their value if once known before." Chaste girls were not only thrifty but more "naturally" female and more fit for both reasons to be wives. Unchaste women might be better suited for romance and sex. Hence the widespread use of mistresses and prostitutes throughout European history.

These fundamental assumptions concerning sex and property never were questioned *widely* in any large civilization before they were challenged in the United States. Compared with most of Europeans, Americans have moved steadily, however slowly, toward a single standard of sexual behavior. For the most part, middle-class Americans have not sanctioned prostitution or even thought it to be desirable. They have had no equivalents of the hetaera of the Greeks, the courtesans of the Romans, the prostitutes of China or their counterparts in Islamic, Hindu, Buddhist or Catholic Latin cultures.

In the United States an anomaly developed. It was expected that young women in the middle classes would remain chaste before marriage. Yet they were accorded a degree of independence unknown elsewhere which permitted them to be much more openly bold in their relations with men. Privately they could experiment and still maintain a reputation for good morals or "thriftiness" as long as they did not lose their virginity. Most incongruous of all in the light of European experience, American middle-class women, despite their independence in flirtation, necking and petting, were treated with extraordinary deference and respect by men. Whereas an explicit sexual double standard in Europe was and is associated with male dominance in all things, a covert and milder sexual double standard in the United States has been accompanied by the elevation of women to romantic heights, almost to worshipful regard.

It was the unprecedented adoption of the principle of free mate choice based on romantic love that promoted both the independence of women and the idealization of them. By the middle of the eighteenth century, marriage had become an affair of the heart for nearly all in the middle classes, although often with parental consent. Writing in the *New England Courant,* young Benjamin Franklin lampooned marriages based on economic interest. Girls who married for such reasons, he charged, were not wed, they were sold. Marriages based on romance dictated that mothers introduce maidens to situations where romance might flourish. The authors of a newspaper article in 1819, long after the principle of free mate choice had been established, complained that mothers often encouraged their daughters of twelve and thirteen years to attend parties and balls. Why not? What an excellent way to introduce them to young men and to teach them how to mix with the opposite sex!

THE SEXUAL REVOLUTION HAS AN EARLY BEGINNING

Everywhere in Europe, peasant girls were expected to be forward, and many became pregnant before marriage, but women from the middle classes would have been utterly shamed if they displayed the boldness shown by American girls of comparable backgrounds. In Colonial America it was impossible to seclude and protect females in the European way. Without chaperones, middle-class young ladies showed somewhat more flexibility with young men than did their sisters across the ocean.

Bundling, which began in the lower classes, was common throughout the Colonies by the middle of the eighteenth century. A Frenchman visiting Connecticut was surprised to find that a chaste woman did not hesitate to share her bed with a male friend, without either of them undressing, in the Colonial version of the older Dutch custom. What once was a practical matter of accommodating overnight guests became an American method of courting. The historic conflict between American Puritan consciences and many opportunities for sexual activity had begun. Puritan ministers railed against bundling; mothers defended it. One verse, written from the young lady's point of view, praised bundling: "If I won't take my sparks to bed, a laughing stock I shall be made," and finally in asking "to be excused," the young lady wondered if she can "e'er married by if bundling be refused?"

The extent of premarital sex is unknown, but to judge from the church records of New England towns, which recorded confessions for premarital fornication between husband and wife, such instances were numerous. The number of confessions went up sharply between 1726 and 1744, a period known now as the Great Awakening, which, very much like our own time, emphasized emotional excitement and honesty in the quest for salvation, and continued up to the Revolution. The records of the church at Groton, Massachusetts, show that of one hundred couples coming to baptize their babies between 1761 and 1775, a third confessed to conceiving their children before marriage. Harvard College had already debated the question "whether it be Fornication to lye with ones Sweetheart before Marriage." Since nearly all the young debaters must have been studying for the ministry (Harvard at that time was a theological school), it seems, clear that the idea of engaged couples having sexual intercourse was widely accepted by the middle of the eighteenth century. Later, when Victorian morality prevailed, it would have been considered outrageous to debate such a principle in public.

"MEDDLING IN SUCH THINGS AS ARE PROPER FOR MEN"

American women began to challenge the traditional perogatives of men in earliest colonial times, although without notable success at first. Governor Winthrop of the Massachusetts Bay Colony believed that the young wife of the Governor of Connecticut had gone insane "by occasion of giving herself wholly to reading and writing," which he considered to be "meddling in such things as are proper for men . . ." When Winthrop's own wife was judged insane, her Puritan women friends attributed the calamity to attempting to act too much like a man. The principal charge against Anne Hutchinson before she was banished from Massachusetts to Rhode Island was that "contrary to Paul, she presumed to instruct men." But even in rigidly patriarchal Puritan New England, men sometimes recognized that women had rights of conscience which must be held inviolate. When one husband tried to forbid his wife from listening to the religious talks of Roger Williams in Rhode Island, he was condemned by members of the church in Providence.

Women were in short supply and becoming more mobile. As time passed, they became more successful in asserting their independence. In 1699 a Rhode Island wife named Rachael Potter left her husband, George, to live in Boston. In order to get her back Mr. Potter promised "to dwell in all loving and quiet behavior," and more to the point, agreed to leave his house, land and moveables to her if he should die. Wives were too valuable to be disposed of lightly. Because women were scarce, widows remarried quickly (Washington, Jefferson and Madison all married widows). Their value in an economy where every hand was useful led many women to become merchants, shopkeepers and even shipowners.

By the early nineteenth century, Europeans particularly were impressed by what seemed to them to be the freer and favored position of women in the new world. In the 1830's, De Tocqueville and others were astounded that American women could travel from one end of the country to the other without being molested. A few years later, Charles Dickens, who otherwise had very little good to say about the United States, was surprised to find the good health and excellent deportment of the independent unmarried young women who worked in the factories of Lowell, Massachusetts. The migrations of young women from middle-class families to industrial towns such as Lowell, Waltham and Lawrence had no precedent in Europe, and what foreigners were seeing was in part the extension to the expanding middle classes in the United States of privileges long granted to upper-class women in Europe. Only aristocratic women dared travel on their own in the old countries, but such travel had become commonplace for middle-class women in America by the early nineteenth century. Although only women of wealth could indulge their tastes for fashion in Europe, the propensity of middle-class women to spend on clothes and furnishings was widespread in the United States.

To the Europeans, American women were not only free, they were pampered. Only in America were audiences addressed as "Ladies and gentlemen" rather than in the reverse order. One mid-century Swiss visitor, observing that the respect of Americans for the female sex was profound, called the country "a women's paradise." Two generations later, an Englishman concluded that "the age of chivalry is not gone. Until America, it never came." American men, he thought, were a puzzle. "They toil and slave. They kill themselves at 40, that their women may live in luxury and become socially and intellectually superior to themselves."

The point of view was male as well as European. In the early nineteenth century, women's education was, as Mrs. John Adams, wife of the second President, had called it in 1778—"narrow" and "contracted," aimed mainly at enabling girls to gain husbands, maintain homes and manage families. More than two hundred finishing schools were established between 1820 and the Civil War to enable women to perform well functions which society thought appropriate to their sex. Religious books, romantic novels, poetry and moral essays were considered particularly suitable for female minds. None of her men teachers would help Susan B. Anthony understand long division. They could not fathom why a girl should insist on mastering it. The first public examination of a girl in geometry in New York in 1829 raised a cry of disapproval and dire warnings against the dissolution of families. When the regents of that state gave to a women's college the right to grant degrees, anger spewed forth from college presidents, sages and popular essayists.

But opportunities for education for American women

far surpassed those in Europe because of the expansion of the public school system, and continuing to insist on meddling in things that previously had been considered fit only for men, women demanded higher education, too. Oberlin College in Ohio (coeducational) opened in 1833; Mt. Holyoke Seminary (for women) in western Massachusetts was incorporated in 1836; and Antioch College in Ohio (coeducational) accepted students in 1853. After the Civil War, when public secondary education became well established, women actually were better educated on the average than men, since more girls than boys were graduated from high schools every year (as has been true ever since). Most Americans continued to think that a college education was appropriate only for men, but within a few decades after the Civil War the major prestige women's colleges were founded in the East so women could get an education in their own schools rather than be intimidated by men in rapidly expanding state-supported coeducational institutions. As early as 1866, *Godey's Lady's Book* proudly reported that there were between three and four hundred women "who hold the full degree of Doctors of Medicine now in successful practice in our Republic," compared with just one in England.

TOWARD EQUAL RIGHTS THROUGH LAW

It was mainly because of education that a growing number of female voices called for more equitable laws and met with less resistance than in Europe. A visiting Englishwoman in 1857 said that "America is full of hopeful signs for women; the men are not so dead set against the rights of women as in the old country . . ." Even in Colonial times, the laws had moved in the direction of equality by providing greater protection for women than had been known in England or elsewhere. In both the Massachusetts Bay Colony and Plymouth, men were forbidden from striking their wives. In all of the New England colonies, laws were enacted to protect the rights of women with regard to their husbands' property, and in New York, where the influence of liberal Dutch law was important, citizens sometimes were appointed to courts to make certain that husbands treated their wives fairly. The implications of the American Revolution and its Declaration of Independence propelled the nation's movement for women's rights still further. Mrs. John Adams warned her husband, one of the authors of the Declaration, that the men of America had better be more generous and favorable to women than their ancestors had been. If not, she predicted, "we are determined to foment a rebellion, and will not hold ourselves down to obey any laws in which we have no right of representation." The honored American battle cry "No taxation without representation" was revived at the first organized women's rights convention at Seneca Falls in western New York State in 1848, which issued a Declaration of Sentiments closely following the first Declaration of Independence, including a provision that women ought not to be taxed unless they had the right to vote.

Having tasted partial emancipation, women in America began to agitate for more on a much larger scale than had been known in Europe. Gradually the Middle and New

England states modified their laws in favor of women, and after the Civil War vast changes in legislation took place aimed at equalizing rights. But the strongest gains were made in the West. Women who had crossed plains and mountains in covered wagons were not likely to think of themselves as weak and inferior. The granting of female suffrage, which had begun quietly in 1838 in the backwoods of Kentucky, where widows rearing children were allowed to vote in school elections, was given strong impetus in 1869 when women began voting on an equal basis with men in the territory of Wyoming. Before the century closed, suffrage had been extended to women in the states of Colorado, Utah and Idaho as well as Wyoming, a privilege established as a right elsewhere only in Sweden, Australia and New Zealand. By 1900, wives in America could own and control their separate property in three-fourths of the states; and in the great majority they could make contracts and bring suit. Legal, social and economic discrimination continued, but the direction Mrs. Adams had indicated more than a hundred years before was being followed at a quickened pace.

A NEW VIEW OF DIVORCE

The 1848 Women's Rights Convention argued that the promise of obedience in the marriage contract was a hideous barbarity that should be abolished. For the first time in history a mass meeting of women assaulted a major assumption of marriage, that women and children had to obey husbands and fathers in order to maintain the stability and welfare of families. Along with the feminist attack on obedience in the marriage vow was a totally new (for a large group) view of divorce. Throughout history divorce was a male prerogative which left women defenseless and in disgrace. But in America radically different conditions permitted a radically new female view toward divorce. Divorcees could travel freely and maintain a good reputation. Where women were scarce, particularly in the West, they had a good chance for remarriage. Slowly, but inexorably, the ideology of independence and equality led to a new female attitude toward divorce. Given proper protection, women began to see divorce not as inevitable disgrace and penury but as an opportunity for freedom and independence.

The question arises: How could divorce become widespread alongside the growing idealization of the family of procreation? It was precisely the idealization of marriage and the nuclear family which prompted couples to go to the divorce court. A young couple marrying for love set up their own homestead; to live apart from one's parents in relative privacy added not just to the independence of the new couple and to the romance of their marriage but placed the burden for making it work entirely on them. The stake in maintaining romance was large, and the difficulty in doing so, considerable. Because the ideals were so high to begin with, disappointments were bound to be deep and conflicts frequently bitter. The American divorce rate has been steady (one divorce to four marriages) in recent years, but it is still about double that for Western Europe. Although divorce is still entirely a male prerogative in many other societies, women initiate legal action in almost seven out of eight divorce cases in the United States. A large proportion of the divorces may not have been desired by the wives, but the very fact that it is considered better form in the United States for women to take the initiative reveals the extent to which this particular manifestation of traditional patriarchy has been destroyed. Compared with women in other countries, the American wife enjoys enormous power in the divorce court. Even in countries where divorce is given with some degree of ease, the wife is rarely awarded alimony if she can work at all; in the United States a divorcee usually gets at least one-third of the husband's annual earnings.

POWER AT HOME

Only a small minority of American men sympathized with the feminist point of view on marriage and motherhood in the nineteenth century. The vast majority were not even concerned, since most middle-class daughters and wives never raised the issue, believing themselves fit only for child-bearing, mothering and spousing. They were not particularly interested in the vote or working outside of the home. They appear to have accepted the American view that women were too pure, if not too weak, to be burdened with higher education or work in the world of men. Some believed, particularly after the Civil War, that women were especially well suited to be teachers (they were paid less than men) or nurses, but that other jobs, in addition to being indelicate, would take women away from their main responsibility as guardian and preserver of morality in the home. Most women agreed. By 1842, Catherine Beecher wrote that in America "the formation of the moral and intellectual character of the young is committed mainly to the female hand." "It was the mother," she asserted, "who formed the character of the future man . . ." After the Civil War the view that the mother was the central, indispensable dispenser of morality and virtue in the family became more pronounced.

What had happened to father? The ambiguity of male authority which had begun in the seventeenth century became more pronounced with the passing of each decade, partly because the young and women asserted their rights to personal independence, but also because the desire of males for independence led them further and further away from the responsibilities of governing families and increasingly into the world of work outside of the home to compete with other males. By the 1840's, De Tocqueville saw that the only powers which father had were those which he could negotiate with other members of his family. Some fifty years later an Englishman observed that while his countrymen were continually going home, American men were continually going to business. At home the American male was sometimes a playmate, occasionally a nullity, less and less an authority. It was at work that he usually made his presence and power felt. In 1912 a writer in a Paris newspaper asserted what other Europeans had been saying and thinking for generations: While the American man rules in the business world, his wife rules at home.

Eventually this power caused many women discomfort. The egalitarian principle clearly had much in its favor: more sexual freedom and pleasure, protection in personal and property rights, the extension of the suffrage, economic power, and educational and occupational opportunities. These were goals which the vast majority of women eventually would espouse. But while women in the nineteenth century first welcomed the assumption of female authority in the training of children, by the middle of the twentieth century many began to wonder how much their own lives had been restricted because of the absence of father.

Traditionally the mother had been forgiving, compassionate, nurturing and protective. Increasingly in America she also became the definer and enforcer of limits. Given the drives for independence among children and the ambiguity of male authority, the tasks of mothering in the middle class grew more arduous with the passing of each generation. In traditional cultures, women could comfortably accept the reflected glory which came via husbands, fathers, brothers and sons, but in America—as the ideology of independence was espoused by women, too—reflected glory meant less and less. Women increasingly wanted to achieve on their own. There were hundreds of thousands of exceptions, of course, as there are today—women who drew deep satisfaction from performing well the varying and always complicated roles of wife and mother. Despite the enormous pressures in the culture for personal independence through achievement, they had learned early to feel comfortable with the extraordinary maternal and wifely responsibilities which had been thrust upon them. They felt good about themselves as persons no matter how often critics might accuse them of being brainwashed. But many others—particularly those with higher education—increasingly and justifiably found that the full-time mothering of aggressive, competitive and rebellious children without much help from father submerged their own individuality.

SUPER MOTHER IN AMERICA

Even in the nineteenth century the anxieties of mothering were especially heavy. In the United States it was believed that the infant was shaped much more by his immediate environment and direct experience than by heredity. What a fantastic undertaking to be a mother in a democracy where every boy can grow up to surpass his father or perhaps even become President! It all depends on how well mother helps him to swim in the swirling currents of social change. In addition to *Godey's Lady's Book*, which had enormous popularity between 1820 and 1860, there were more than sixty women's magazines by 1850 which, along with manuals for child care and home management, were dedicated at least in part to helping mother meet her grave responsibilities. Poems and prize-winning essays of the period often emphasized the vital importance to the young child of every word, glance or move which mother made. In good American fashion, mothers were warned not to be overly protective; they were also reminded that children learned through imitation and that the mother's behavior would be the single greatest influence on the moral character of the young. To be super mother in America brought mounting anxieties, particularly since the rules of parenting were constantly changing and young mothers, separated much more from their own mothers and aunts than in other cultures, lacked help and training in child-rearing. Much anxiety was associated with the issue of independence. Mothers wanted their children to become independent because the culture told them that was right, but they also wanted to keep them from getting into trouble because their instincts told them that that was right. Young boys should be allowed to do daring things but they should not get hurt. Adolescent girls should be venturesome but not get pregnant. Is it any wonder that inconsistency often resulted?

Mothers are still confused (and inconsistent) because they want their children to achieve, as the culture tells them, while also wanting their children to be happy. Almost every middle-class mother knows these pressures well. They check report cards, attend back-to-school classes or PTA meetings for their children, and confer with the teachers. They want their children to do well in school, and they also want them to go to dancing class, be good at athletics, and take advantage of teenage play facilities at the church or community center. Life for mother is one endless whirl of activity as keeper of the schedule, chauffeur, and yea- and nay-sayer with respect to those enterprises which must be negotiated. A lack of training, constantly changing ground rules, guilt, and the sheer volume of work and choices make it a wonder that American middle-class mothers do as well as they do. With the decline in the fathers' authority, mothers became the obvious target for the desire of children to test limits. Shouts and even blows directed by small children against mom are common. But the tensions caused for super mother by aggressive children in the absence of father has been an American phenomenon for many generations. In a typical pattern of difficulty and misunderstanding between spouses, mother wishes father would take a more active hand in disciplining the children, wonders why he does not show more initiative and resents having to ask him. Father wonders why, after a hard day's work, mother hasn't achieved greater control of the household. Why are children disrespectful? Why does she seem so tired after being home all day? Mother feels guilty for intruding (or wanting to intrude) on father's quiet time at home, knowing how hard he works. Yet she wonders about the excitement and pleasure in his work, too. Does he meet interesting friends and flirt with other women? Father feels guilty for wanting to leave the noise and confusion at home. Yet he wonders if he isn't entitled to more time away with the boys or more compassionate female companionship. Little recognition is given to how much tension between them is caused by the demands which "independent" youngsters make on mother. Moving separately in two emotional spheres, husband and wife tend to become less aware of the emotional needs of the other.

AMERICAN HUSBANDS AND MOTHEROLOTRY

Judged from the point of view of wives, husbands are often too busy and uncommunicative; their preoccupation with work is resented. Yet for generations American mothers have pushed their sons toward achievement as a way of expressing their individuality. Weaned on McGuffey's *Reader* in the nineteenth century which told little boys that if they worked hard they could reach the goals of wealth, usefulness and happiness, many men later discovered that wealth and even usefulness did not always bring happiness. The strains of competition are enormous, and then, too, there is the pressure to go beyond one's past achievements. By middle age, many apparently successful American men begin to wonder what success really is. What often matters most is what *you* feel about your own worth. The best of surgeons, lawyers and poets know better than society how far below their achievements are the standards set by themselves. The pressure is there to be better than any man; but the internal pressure is there, too, the nagging, paralyzing doubt that nothing one does is really good enough. Middle age for many men, even those with high status and income in the middle classes, is a time of fatigue and disappointment.

It is usually in middle age and sometimes earlier, when men feel burdened by the strain of work and unsupported emotionally by their wives, that they begin to mythologize about their own boyhood and wonderful mothers. How much better to be a young boy in America, truly independent and carefree with dreams untarnished than to be successful but burdened by responsibilities and work. "Let the million-dollared ride!" wrote John Greenleaf Whittier, "the bare-foot boy at his side is much happier." And why not? Longfellow remembered "the boyhood's painless play" whose health mocks the doctor's rules. After all, "a boy's will is the wind's will." Even before he was twenty, Edgar Allan Poe wrote of boyhood as a summer sun "Whose waning is the dreariest one / For all we live to know is known / And all we seek to keep hath flown."

The very same men who as adolescents were so anxious to be free from their mothers' houses remember in middle age that the most important person in their truly happy days—the time of cookie jars, good-night kisses, favorite meals and exciting stories—was, of course, mother. Critics of the twentieth century have written of "momism" and of the overbearing, overprotective and stifling kind of mothering which produces neurosis in sons and daughters. But in the nineteenth century, particularly in the latter half, conventional wisdom went the other way. Although wives were difficult, mothers were wise and pure. Motherolotry appeared in the poetry not only of Whittier, Lowell, Oliver Wendell Holmes and lesser poets of sentiment but also of such an unlikely poet as Poe. Mothers became a symbol as well as a guardian of morality in the poetry and essays of the time. Lowell valued "More than Plato things I learned / At that best academy, a mother's knee." Whittier, looking "across the years" saw himself beside "my mother's knee." Nathaniel P. Willis, a minor but popular poet, wrote that "in his better moments" the "Years and sin and manhood flee/ And leave me at my mother's knee." Most soldiers had wives or sweethearts in the Civil War, but they were rarely mentioned in the popular songs of the time. Instead one finds such song titles as "Angel Mother, I'm Coming Home," "Be My Mother till I Die," "Dear Mother, I Have Come Home to Die," "If I Sleep, Will Mother Come," "Is That Mother Bending o'er Me?" and "Kiss Me Before I Die, Mother."

PATRIARCHY, NO; COMPETITION, YES!

Motherolotry continued into the twentieth century, when Mother's Day became a time of familial (and commercial) activity second only to Christmas. But men no longer called their own wives "Mother." Motherolotry was likely to be resented by young wives and mothers trying to manage their own precocious, rebellious children without much help from their husbands. Yet there are probably few women who realize the extent to which the common pattern of mutual resentment and recrimination between husbands and wives is linked to the decline of patriarchy and the ensuing struggle for independence and equality by each family member.

Whether one sees the struggle through the characters of Edgar Lee Masters' *Spoon River Anthology*, radio and television soap operas, twentieth-century novels on domestic life or the works of contemporary playwrights, such as Albee, Inge, Williams, or Miller, the scenario deals with the male–female struggle to assert and protect individual independence. Whereas the wife may see her husband's work as adventuresome and stimulating, he is more likely to feel it is fatiguing and stressful. While she may see him as a little boy grown into a big boy emotionally dependent on her as he was on his mother, he may be missing badly the caretaking which men have received at home for centuries in return for protecting and providing for the family. While she may be feeling the need to assert a self that is lost in a myriad of roles as wife and mother, he may think that she is already overly assertive, bossy and even controlling. To judge from the popular comic strips of the twentieth century, that is exactly how many men do feel. Several studies of family and adventure comics reveal that competition with wives is debilitating: when men marry they not only lose their power, they also lose their hair and become fat; they actually shrink (while single men are invariably taller than their female friends, half of the time married women are as tall or taller than their husbands); hostile actions are more frequently initiated by wives than husbands; and women accomplish what they set out to do, while men are thwarted in the majority of cases; the unmarried male is an adventurer, a test pilot, a cowboy or athlete who has amazing prowess—once married, he often becomes weak and ineffectual.

The comics reflect the defensiveness of married men, but competition between the sexes before marriage appears to have put males on the defensive, too. With the decline of patriarchy, their citadels—colleges, clubs and even barrooms—have been invaded. To judge from the movies, popular literature and case histories recorded on the couches of clinicians, sexual initiative has frequently passed to girls. As already indicated, defensive reactions are commonplace, including a spate of television ads which show men how to keep or restore their masculinity. One of the most blatant, sponsored by a leading spray deodorant in 1967, showed a square-jawed male face looking down from the top of the screen at the delicate face of a demure female. After smacking his fist into a brick wall and saying, "Pow—" the male asserted, "I'm twice the man you are." She responded in a fragile voice, "You're wonderful!" This particular spray deodorant, the viewers were told, gave twice the power of other deodorants. When the girl asked, "Don't you like perfume?" the square-jawed male answered, "I like power!" Zam! Boom! He banged the wall again; she whispered once more, "You're wonderful."

WHAT DO THEY WANT?

It is hardly surprising that American men are defensive and confused. Of course, there are exceptions, men who welcome with zest the sexual boldness of women. Those are the swingers, who, in exploiting sexual opportunities, often make so-called liberated women utterly dependent on their erratic behavior. But a much larger number of American men are puzzled, making Freud's famous question about the female, "What do they want?," quite personal for them.

College girls and married women, too, confuse their male partners by asserting their independence and equality while complaining about male passivity. They seem to be saying, "We want to be independent and equal but we want males to be strong, too." When I ask girls in my course on the family to state the qualities they most desire in husbands, they usually prefer gentleness, compassion, understanding and other qualities connected with love and respect in marriage. When asked to choose those characteristics which they desire most in a male, they list strength, aggressiveness, and even use the word "commanding." Even women who think of themselves as strong women's liberationists complain that their boyfriends or husbands are not assertive enough in bed.

Clearly, most modern women do not want the exaggerated defensive male reaction portrayed in the deodorant commercial on television described above. They do want males who have a sense of their own strength as persons even as they want more independence for themselves. How could it be otherwise? As Americans, they have been taught to assert their independence; as females, their bio-cultural inheritance prompts them to look for strong (protective and perhaps commanding) males. Millions of years of biological and cultural selection cannot be obliterated even by the Declaration of Independence or the use of birth-control pills.

Just as the 1960's presented adolescents of both sexes with distinctively new experiences that shaped a negative reaction to productivity and achievement values, that decade also brought a new consciousness to women that older values guiding male–female relationships were at least partly wrong. Because of truly radical advances in contraception, as well as higher education and the change from a production to a service economy, women developed a new way of thinking about their own bodies and minds. Just as older generations feel under attack and have difficulty in adjusting to the new perceptions and feelings of the young, males also are feeling attacked and disoriented by the new attitudes of women. Just as the young have a clearer, surer sense of what they don't want while struggling in confusion toward some new values to guide them, women, certain that the old ways are wrong, also seem to speak in many tongues and voices about the meaning of their new consciousness. But certain themes emerge as central. Women want more control over their own bodies and minds than they have ever had before. They may not be certain of all the implications of what they desire or be willing to accept them, but there can be no question as to the direction in which they want to move. Their new consciousness and aspirations do not constitute a female problem. They are part of the human problem and, in some respects, a peculiarly American problem: the conflict between the desire for independence and for dependable loving relations in families.

WOMEN AND THEIR BODIES

Nowhere is the problem more serious in America than in the middle-class marriages where women, as well as men, now commonly have sex outside of marriage as a way of exercising their independence. More often than not, according to Kinsey and others, hard-working, middle-aged husbands become less interested in sex at the very time that freedom from mothering, experience in sex and reliable contraception stimulate their wives' interest to new heights. Tired of the heavy responsibility of disciplining children, feeling taken for granted and neglected, the middle-aged woman often is drawn beyond sexual fantasy. Since the 1960's, according to post-Kinsey studies, in what appears to be the sharpest change in the pattern of American sexual behavior, she enters increasingly into affairs outside of marriage as a way of showing her independence. Seeking love and affirmation of her worth as a person, and feeling free to control and express her own body as women in previous generations could not, she now looks to sex for both.

Commonly, middle-aged males have engaged in extramarital sexual affairs, but their behavior was not nearly as threatening to the stability of families as the newly expressed sexuality of women. Now many men find the expression of new sexuality by their wives in extramarital relationships to be hostile if not disabling. Absorbed in his work, struggling to succeed, the husband between thirty-five and forty-five wants stability at home. Just when his need for succor is greatest he is faced with his wife's search for a new self which also involves her growing sense of sexuality. Understanding the legitimacy of the desire by women to control and express their own bodies, he may be no less shaken when his own wife does so outside of marriage.

It is not clear that the sharp increase in female extramarital sex is responsible for the growing percentage of divorcing couples in middle age. But the most outstanding change in the pattern of divorce in the last decade has not been its overall increase; what is most striking has been the growing percentage of divorcing couples with children, 60 percent in 1970 versus 42 percent in 1948, when the overall divorce rate was actually slightly higher. Fourteen percent of the divorces in 1970 came in marriages that had already survived more than twenty years.

While consciousness of the possibility of controlling and expressing one's own body is now widespread in the women's movement for independence and equality, it is far from new. Feminists in the eighteen-forties and fifties made war on corsets and wore bloomers, Turkish-styled pantaloons, named for Amelia Bloomer, one of their number who wore them all the time. In the 1920's, when Victorian modes of fashion received their sharpest criticism, women bound their breasts and adopted a boyish figure to symbolize their aspirations for independence in the use of their bodies. That extremist feminists burn brassieres today and millions of women wear pants and men's shirts no more signifies their desire to be boys than did the fashion of bloomers or bobbed hair in other times. What is different about the contemporary female fashions is that they are accompanied by a much stronger and more widespread desire to have sexual experiences before and outside of the marital relationship.

WOMEN AND THEIR MINDS

The birth-control pill became available in 1960, at the very time that it became commonplace for young women in the middle classes to go to college, and increasingly to coeducational institutions. While more than one-third of the eight million young people enrolled in colleges today are women, less than one-tenth of the college students in 1910 were female. Since that time the rate of increase for women entering and graduating from college consistently outpaced that for men, but women did not necessarily pursue a career. In fact, the proportion of women in the professions went down in the 1950's. But in the 1960's there was a sharp increase over the previous decade in the percentage of women relative to men entering graduate schools and professional schools.

Equalization of higher educational opportunities has been followed by a growing desire on the part of women to use their brains in the world of work outside of household management. Studies of Vassar alumnae showed that most women who graduated in the 1940's preferred to center their lives on the home, with some outside interests. The classes of 1954 to 1958 revealed a shift in emphasis: home was important but with a career fitted around it. But the classes of 1964 to 1966 voted for "career with as little time out for family as possible."

The differences arise from two major factors related to breakthroughs in postgraduate educational opportunities: effective birth control which enables women to postpone having children; and fundamental changes in the nature of work in America. In the 1960's, for the first time in the history of any society, more people were working at the exchange of goods and services than in the production of them. Of the nearly fourteen million jobs that developed in the sixties, women took almost two-thirds of them. They now make up more than 60 percent of all service workers, compared with less than 40 percent before World War II. By 1970 more than 43 percent of all women were in the labor force, contrasted to only 23 percent in 1920. There is absolutely no known biological reason why women cannot be professors, journalists, advertising executives, bankers, lawyers or doctors. Of course, few of them hold such positions, and there was actually a drop in the proportion of women engaged in several professions in the 1950's. But the next decade introduced a new era in which large numbers of college-educated women began to think of professional and business careers much as men have done for generations. A service economy opens up many other kinds of jobs, too, which do not rely on muscle power as much as on skills which are equally available to intelligent men and women: program computers, barbers, train conductors, taxi drivers, traffic police and so on. Such jobs do not necessarily present intellectual challenges, but they do give women an opportunity for more extensive adult contact and possible collaboration with others in solving problems outside the home.

Chances are nine out of ten that a girl born this year will at some time be gainfully employed. There is probably an even chance that she will work after she is married. More than one-third of mothers in the United States are now in the labor force at least part time. What is more startling is that one-fourth of the working wives have children under three; one-third have children under five; and one-half of the mothers of school-age children are now in the labor force. But the growing opportunity at work resulting partly from higher education in upper-middle-class women and partly from the impetus to earn money in less well-to-do women does not mean the end of discrimination against women in employment. For all the American emphasis on equality, women have been less able to reach positions of power and prestige in the United States than in several other countries (for example, there is a higher proportion of women doctors in England and of female jurists in France)—a condition which an increasing number of them find intolerable.

Young college-educated women who wish to have an independent career face problems no less perplexing and undoubtedly more commonplace than those which middle-aged women feel as a result of their heightened sexuality and desire for work away from the home. Although an increasing number of young women are willing to postpone marriage, many still desire early marriage. A majority of those who marry do not want to stand in the way of their husbands' ambitions in graduate school and professional work or business. Most still want children and the responsibility that goes with mothering; but they also want to stretch their minds in challenging work outside of the home. The typical compromise, unlike the answer given by the 1964–1966 Vassar graduates, is to postpone work until the children are well into school. But what kind of job can a middle-aged college-educated woman find which is commensurate with her talents? What skills does she have? How does she gain the confidence to compete in the world of work? Does she go back to school? At that point, many women enter into what sociologist Ruth Useem has called a "second adolescence," with a renewed interest in the struggle for identity. Having "served" as wife and mother, she now may need distance from her family. Whereas "making it on one's own" in first adolescence mainly meant getting away from her parents and home, marrying and having children, it now means moving into the world of work outside of her own home, being respected for competence in work and accepted as an independent person apart from her marital and family ties ("Oh, you are Mrs. so-and-so," or, "You're Jane's mother").

EQUALITY: BIOLOGY AND CULTURE

The preoccupation with personal independence is an American cultural phenomenon. It is an emphasis which may lead women and men away from the more important issue: How does one feel good about one's self? Some women relish nursing their infants for more than a year. Some love to bake and sew. There are women who even enjoy polishing silver and ironing; and many still take great pleasure in the accomplishments of their husbands and children. Such women ought not to be told that they have failed to grow as persons any more than the women who are happy driving a taxi or running a large business ought to be scorned as unfeminine.

What is considered manly and womanly varies to some extent from culture to culture, as Margaret Mead showed many years ago. Now we are in a period of great flux in American society. Courses in home economics have been opened to boys and many are enjoying learning how to bake and knit. Investment houses advertise for female account executives, and the number of women in high management positions has grown significantly if not spectacularly in the last few years. That does not mean, as many liberationists of both sexes now assert, that roles have nothing to do with biology and are merely cultural impositions.

Biology and culture continually interact in shaping the behavior of women and men in any society. We saw earlier in this book how postnatal fatherhood—clearly a cultural invention—probably grew out of a series of biological developments. We also speculated as to how cultural fatherhood led to patriarchy and how patriarchy was rationalized to justify the arbitrary subordination and exploitation of females. Finally, we have seen how the historic movement of American women to assert their independence has led to a growing attack on their traditional roles as mothers and wives.

THE DIFFERENCES THAT BIOLOGICAL DIFFERENCES MAKE

The critical question, of course, is how much of what we think of as female is rooted in biology? How much can be explained by culture?

Many researchers in varied fields are now investigating the biological bases of differences in female–male behavior. When consistent patterns of difference in behavior between the sexes, particularly in infants and small children, are found in *many cultures*, it is likely that they have some basis in evolutionary biology. When those behavioral differences and the roles connected with them can be directly related to differences in body structure or physiology, it is even more probable that biological factors underlie them.

Researchers also look for corroborative or contradictory evidence in the study of primates and contemporary hunter-gatherer societies. There is a tendency on the part of some psychologists and anthropologists, as well as polemicists for women's liberation, to dismiss the study of primates as irrelevant to an understanding of human behavior. But evidence such as that which shows young primate females to be not as aggressive as males seems significant when those same differences are found between human males and females.

Also, since *Homo sapiens* spent about 99 percent of his and her existence as hunters and gatherers,* evidence from societies such as those of the Kung Bushmen in the Kalihari desert or the Australian aborigines is important in helping us to understand the cultural and biological past of modern man and woman. Significant findings of behavioral and role differences between males and females in modern societies cannot reasonably be dismissed as

---

* Ninety percent of the eighty billion people who ever inhabited the earth were hunter-gatherers.

recent cultural impositions when they are also found in hunter-gatherer societies.

The truth about biologically based behavioral differences between males and females—insofar as it is known —never should be used as an excuse for the exploitation of one sex by the other; but the closer we come to the truth, the nearer we will come to fulfilling our common humanity. My own view, as will be shown in the last chapter, is that much can and should be done to modify male–female roles in American families, including a return to more authoritative fathering. But no matter how strong one's opinions for or against the demand for new roles, it is wrong to ignore the growing evidence of important biologically based differences in the behavior of males and females.

The data can be found mostly in scientific journals, but fortunately for those who want to see such material put together in book form, there are now three important books on the subject. The first, by anthropologist Ashley Montagu, updated in a 1968 version, appeared in 1952 under the title *The Natural Superiority of Women*. The main point of the book, now overwhelmingly supported by studies in many cultures, is that females are physically healthier, mentally more stable and generally more resilient than males. A second extremely important book appeared in 1966 under the editorship of Eleanor Maccoby entitled *The Development of Sex Differences*. Dr. Maccoby, a psychologist with considerable methodological and statistical sophistication, provides at the end of the book an annotated bibliography on 577 studies bearing on the question of sex-linked differences in behavior.

Dr. Maccoby does not try to explain behavioral differences in terms of biology; that task was undertaken more recently in a book by psychologist Judith M. Bardwick called *Psychology of Women* (published in 1970). In it, Dr. Bardwick unequivocally argues that prenatal hormonal sensitizing of the brain predisposes the two sexes to different conditioning in any culture. From the evidence presented, there can be little question that Dr. Bardwick is correct in arguing that there are congenital, biochemical factors which provide different biological settings for the development of the two sexes. An unsolved problem remains. Which behavioral differences can be ascribed to which biochemical differences? Today, tough-minded investigators are hard at work at many research centers throughout the world, but particularly in the United States, on just that question. We are on the frontiers of research, and conclusive answers to many significant questions about sexual differences are not yet available.

However, there are several statements which can be made about male–female differences that appear to be based on structural, hormonal or neurological differences between the sexes at birth and which also fit the theory that human males and females adapted biologically and culturally through role specialization to promote the survival of the maximum number of offspring. As previously discussed, nature promoted the survival of the human species by encouraging sexual dimorphism in humans to help them provide more effective care for relatively helpless infants. Other differences with behavioral implications also can be explained by nature's interest in human survival.

First, as already noted, females are healthier than males. They have lower rates of fetal and infant mortality at every age (in only four or five countries of the world do males outlive females, and in each case there is a specific cultural explanation). Death from almost all causes comes to males earlier, with the exception, of course, of deaths resulting from disorders related to reproduction. For dozens of diseases—from Parkinson's to congenital deafness and even to lung cancer (according to a hormonal study reported in 1971)—disproportionate male vulnerability to illness can be attributed to biological differences in the two sexes. Studies in many countries also show that even when the illness rate is higher among females, they recover much more quickly and frequently than males. Nature obviously has a huge stake in keeping females healthy because, while human pregnancy lasts so long, it usually results in only a single helpless infant. Mothers have to adapt to unusual hormonal and anatomical changes during pregnancy and, in all but recent times, be healthy enough to suckle their young effectively for two or three years after if a wet nurse is not available.

A second difference easily explained by the theory of natural selection is that females everywhere in the world mature earlier than males. The earlier physical maturity of girls, except in muscular development, even extends to height—girls at age eleven shoot ahead of boys and grow rapidly until they are fifteen. At age nine, girls are about eighteen months ahead of boys in rate of bone development and growth of permanent teeth, and, of course, females arrive at puberty earlier than males. Reproductive efficiency is well served by having females mature earlier. They are more likely to become pregnant several times while still relatively young and be strong enough to take care of their offspring, and they are more likely to live long enough to see their children through to their own childbearing years.

The third difference is that most human females cease ovulating in their late forties (menopause is unknown in other animals), while males remain virile (in one recorded case up to the age of a hundred and nineteen). Nature decided that female *Homo sapiens* could not be allowed to bear children at an age when childbearing became more risky. Even if they survived childbirth, mothers who had their babies much later would not be likely to live long enough for the unusually prolonged caretaking which human offspring require. By permitting older females to escape the hazards of childbirth, nature gave them a longer lease on life. For a species which depends on the accumulation of knowledge and wisdom to survive, there is good reason to prolong life, especially that of females who are the custodians of knowledge when it comes to child care. Because older women are protected from the dangers of pregnancy and childbirth, caretaking resources are multiplied through aunts, grandmothers, midwives and female friends.

A fourth difference is that while human females arrive at puberty earlier than males, they do not seem to be driven to frequent sexual arousal and activity as early as males. The Kinsey studies and many others show that boys have strong genital drives in their early teens and even as early as age eight. Here, many readers will say, "Ah, that is cultural!" Undoubtedly the heightened sexual activity of young boys in the Western world is partly cultural, as the sexual precocity of young females in Polynesia and Melanesia would seem to indicate.

But there are also anatomical and physiological reasons for the earlier sexuality of boys. Because the penis (which is much larger than its female counterpart, the clitoris) lies outside the body, it is subject to frequent stimulation from clothes, changes in bodily position (even in three-week-old babies) and pressure from the bladder. Mothers have long observed that the penis is one of the small boy's first toys; and it has been found that normal young adult males have erect penises during more than half of their dreaming time while asleep (although the content of the dream probably is not sexual most of the time). The genitals of females are less conspicuous. The clitoris of the infant girl may be bathed but it is rarely touched, pointed to or named. Awareness of genital tumescence comes much later in females than males, perhaps as late as between age eight and thirteen on the average. In addition, nature has arranged to give nearly all human females a hymen in what Margaret Mead suggests was an effort to discourage early genitality. Whatever the reason, there is no male homologue for the hymen. While it is now clear, as a result of the studies by Masters and Johnson, that it is the clitoris and not the vagina which is the center of erotic genital response in females, it is possible that the hymen serves as an inhibitor of early sexual activity in the form of intercourse. Hormones may also discourage early orgasmic experience for females. When males are given estrogens (female hormones) for special reasons, they usually report a loss of sexual desire, but when females are given testosterone (male hormone) treatments, they frequently experience stronger sexual arousal.

Evidently nature intended that as female hominids evolved they should enjoy genital sex when they grew older and more experienced, but nature also discouraged early genital activity which would have disassociated sex from childbearing. It would not have been in the interest of survival for very young females to be continually aroused sexually in hunter-gatherer societies. Better that their energies should be concentrated on supporting intrauterine life and relatively helpless offspring. One can see how natural selection works. There was nothing in the *reproductive* physiology of females which required an orgasm, but those hominid males who could not ejaculate sperm left no descendants. Orgasmic capacity in males was rewarded. Males, who were frequently away hunting, would contribute more efficiently to the reproduction of the species not only if they desired sex whenever the opportunity arose but also if they were capable of having an orgasm.

As noted earlier, much has been discovered since Kinsey concerning female sexuality, and there can be no argument with those who insist that Victorian prudery and morality—truly cultural impositions which go far beyond any biological mandate—probably have been responsible for frigidity and unresponsiveness in many women in Western societies. Indeed, Dr. Mary Jane Sherfey, in her book *The Nature and Evolution of Female Sexuality*, hypothesizes on the basis of physiological evidence concerning the virtual insatiability of clitoral orgasmic response in many females that as recently as 12000 to 8000 B.C., it was females and not males who were in a constant state of sexual excitement and desire. She reasons that males may have forcefully suppressed the inordinate sexual demands of females following the domestication of animals and the introduction of agricultural life in order to promote the survival of many children and to establish clear kinship lines. But surely nature has been interested in the promotion of the survival of many children for far longer than ten thousand years. If it was the introduction of family bonds which inhibited female sexuality, those restraints were imposed at least thirty-five thousand years ago, according to fossil remains of Cro-Magnon man.

The theory of natural selection provides a simpler, clearer explanation for the postponement of female genital sexuality than Dr. Sherfey's, and it is supported by what is known today of hunter-gatherers as well as by primate ethology. Males show more persistent earlier orgasmic activity than females. Dr. Sherfey herself points out that many women experienced their first coital orgasm only after their first pregnancy for what is probably physiological as well as psychological reasons. In all women, as long as there is no obstetrical damage, pregnancies increase the volume of sexual edema and enhance the capacity for sexual tension, thereby increasing the capacity for sexual pleasure.

The failure of an ovulated egg to become fertilized in the creation of new life appears to bring considerable difficulty to most females because of hormonal changes in the several days preceding menstruation. While premenstrual tension has long been a subject of uninformed discussion, it is now known from studies in many cultures that females experience marked tension, depression, fatigue, abdominal bloating, allergies, backaches and even psychotic symptoms during the premenstrual period. Studies in France and England reveal that approximately three-fourths of the crimes committed by females in those countries are clustered in the premenstrual period along with suicides, accidents, a decline in the quality of school-work and in intelligence scores and visual acuity. Emotional cycles have also been observed in males, but the evidence is not systematic or clearly related to hormonal activity. With females, it is possible that nature may be commenting through hormonal activity on the failure to conceive. There are other possibilities, too. Perhaps premenstrual tension was not a factor in the lives of hominid females one or two million years ago when, if Dr. Sherfey is correct, they may have experienced almost continual orgasmic experience in something analogous to heat in other mammals during the last days of the menstrual cycle (even today, according to Kinsey, roughly 90 percent of American women prefer sexual relations during the fourteen days before menstruation, often called the luteal phase of the cycle). The unsatisfied sexual propensities of females when pelvic edema and congestion is great provide another plausible explanation for premenstrual tension. Whatever the ultimate cause, hormonal changes are the immediate triggers to the now well-documented cyclical differences in behavior between males and females.

Biological (as well as cultural) conditioning probably is responsible for a fifth major behavioral difference found consistently in many studies in several cultures: females have a greater propensity than males for socially responsive behavior. Females of all ages, in nearly all of the studies made, show that they care more about people and what others think of them. Totally reliable measures have not been found for studying qualities of sociability in small infants, but there is important research which shows that females at birth have more sensitivity to touch and at six months greater preference for a human face than do males. At thirteen months, girls show a stronger response than boys to variations in the inflection of adult voices and also manifest a greater variety of voice inflection to communicate feelings and moods. Judith Bardwick suggests that such differences probably are due to differences in the central nervous and endocrine systems of females and males at birth. She acknowledges that such biological predispositions tend to be reinforced in all cultures. That appears to be the case, according to Beatrice and John Whiting, who, in studying children three to six years of age in six different cultures (including the United States), found that girls are consistently more sociable and boys more aggressive in relations with others. When Eleanor Maccoby reported on twenty-two studies measuring one aspect of sociability—showing interest and positive feelings for others—statistically significant differences between the sexes were shown in twenty-one of them in favor of girls (there was no difference in only one study). That preschool girls display many more themes of affection in doll play than boys, or that girls age two to four draw and talk about persons more than boys, may be attributed by some to cultural conditioning only; but in the face of the Whiting evidence, studies of primates, infant studies and what is known about differences in the endocrinology of males and females, biology also seems to be quite important in predisposing females toward sociability.

The opposite of female sociability is male aggression. The male hormone, testosterone, clearly appears to be related to aggressive behavior. Although male and female infants begin life with nearly equal amounts of testosterone, the quantity of the hormone increases more rapidly in boys than girls during adolescence. There is abundant evidence that the dramatic increase in testosterone levels in adolescent boys accounts for their heightened aggressive (and, as already stated, libidinal) behavior. When male and female primates are given additional testosterone, they show much more aggressive behavior than previously. That small boys are much more physically active than small girls will come as no surprise to nearly all mothers. Almost every study of females and males of all ages, including more than a dozen from ages two or three to five or six show that males imitate aggression more, project aggression in doll play more, or act more aggressively than females without being stimulated or encouraged to imitate or project their feelings. Even if the explanation for male aggression does not rest in male–female differences in the central nervous system or in hormone physiology, biological factors, including muscular strength, body structure and energy capacity could account for the hyperactivity and aggressive behavior of boys. Culture undoubtedly reinforces such biological predispositions as muscle or energy capacity, and biological factors themselves may change over hundreds of thousands of years because of cultural conditioning. For example, it is possible that males have a larger number of red corpuscles to carry nourishment to their cells than do females because of their larger energy requirements.

Perhaps it is even mainly culture which makes females more sociable than males and boys more aggressive than their sisters. Margaret Mead found the women of the cannibalistic Mundugumor of New Guinea to be as assertive as their men in 1932, when that small group was in a state of disintegration. She also found that Tchambuli women in New Guinea, numbering only a few hundred, did many "masculine" things, such as fishing, while the males, who decorated themselves, carved, painted and danced, seemed less responsible and more emotionally dependent than the females. But these cases, concerning unusually small and, often, dying cultures are the exceptions, and there is a perfectly sensible explanation in the theory of natural selection for females and males having biological propensities which lead to the differences described above.

Infants require responsive as well as healthy mothers. At least, before the advent of bottle-feeding they needed responsive adult females to assume the role of mother and to nurse them. Many studies show that responsiveness to small infants by mother or mother substitutes—touching, nuzzling, smiling, hugging—is extremely important to the development of youngsters as healthy human beings.

The survival of the species throughout most of hominid life was probably also enhanced by making males more adventuresome and aggressive than females. On the hunt, males would explore new territory, attack big game and be more courageous in fighting off predators; they would also compete more vigorously for available females, thereby winnowing out the weaker males in the process of natural selection. If, as studies show, small boys—even those six to eighteen months of age—stray further from their mothers than girls do and generally seem to be more exploratory as well as aggressive, those traits may derive from thousands of generations of hominid hunting when such qualities would have been rewarded by survival itself.

The boundary lines between nature and nurture often seem blurred, as in the studies showing consistent differences between the sexes in learning abilities. There is no doubt that girls develop language ability generally and verbal ability specifically much earlier in infancy than boys and that males show higher ability in mathematical and spatial reasoning than females, at least from four or five years of age on. Girls articulate speech more clearly and earlier than boys and use longer sentences at earlier ages, while boys do better at spatial tasks. The question is, Why?

One perfectly sensible hypothesis is that mothers talk to their infant daughters more than they do to their infant sons. That is just what two studies revealed in 1967 and 1971. But perhaps the real reason that mothers talk to girl infants more is that they get more response, as two researchers showed in 1971 when they found that girl infants reacted more to auditory signals than boys.

Why should girl infants respond earlier? Another reasonable hypothesis has been suggested by psychologist Jerome Kagan, a leading student of infant behavior. Perhaps the left hemisphere of the brain in females, which controls language ability, develops precociously in females, making girls more disposed to use language to organize and communicate their experience, while boys compensate with the development of the right hemisphere which controls spatial reasoning. If this hypothesis is correct, it should not be expected that there will be great female geometricians, musicians or chess players in any culture (actually the case thus far) no matter how strongly the American egalitarian ideal takes hold. On the other hand, the number of truly great female poets, novelists, anthropologists, lawyers and doctors (already disproportionately high when compared with the number of composers, mathematicians, engineers or architects) should go up as opportunities are more widely opened to women.

If natural selection has favored the species by promoting in males and females different biologically based behavioral characteristics which—while not immutable—are rooted deeply in their natures, the roles and functions which in part derive from those characteristics will not be changed easily by writing constitutions, making speeches or even by eliminating sexual stereotyping in children's literature. Ideology, even supported by a bottle formula and birth-control pills, cannot successfully defy the biological consequences of our evolutionary history entirely. Polemicists for women's liberation, no matter how angry, should not be allowed to ignore what can be inferred reasonably about the biological basis of differences in the behavior of males and females.

But that does not mean that the defenders of an essentially biological explanation of behavioral and role differences in males and females should ever use the theory of natural selection to exploit and oppress females. Sexist advertising, discrimination in employment, the suppression of talent in girls to please boys and the downgrading of women's tasks as wife and mother have hurt countless numbers of females and society as a whole. As the work of psychologist Matina Horner, sociologist Alice Rossi and others show, there are many subtle patterns of cultural conditioning which have no necessary basis in biology but which deny women the right to control their own minds and bodies. Fortunately, although we are affected by it, we are not imprisoned by nature's design, which is constantly changing. Moreover, cultural variations in male–female roles do exist, and studies showing consistent behavioral differences between the sexes deal only in statistical probabilities, not individual cases. Large numbers of males and females who deviate from the norm should be respected for their essential humanity.

Because *Homo sapiens* is a learning species, it is not totally dependent on biological inheritance. Natural selection may have dictated the evolution of patriarchy, but it is possible to alter the traditional meaning of that term so that rule by fathers no longer implies domination of females by males. While our hunter-gatherer inheritance cannot be ignored, we are no longer hunter-gatherers, and we have it within our power—at least to some extent—to determine the kind of roles we wish to have as women and men, and as I will argue later, the kind of families we wish to have.

There is nothing against nature's laws which makes it necessarily harmful for a man to carry out the garbage—although European men were shocked to find American men doing it in the mid-nineteenth century—or for a woman to assume a position on top of her husband in sexual intercourse. The important question is what these activities mean to the spouses. Nor is there anything in nature which should prevent women from performing in a variety of occupations more effectively than they do now in the United States. In Russia there are women who are excellent carpenters, plumbers, industrial managers, machinists and railroad locomotive engineers, as well as surgeons and lawyers, although even in the Soviet Union the important managerial, professional and political positions are nearly always held by men, and the child-care positions are held by women.

I hope it is clear that I believe that individual women

are fit for any occupation of importance, including the Presidency of the United States or the Secretary-General-ship of the United Nations, and that women must be given the opportunity to perform in these capacities. It seems ridiculous to argue that premenstrual tension, of which most women are at least aware, would keep them from being good Presidents or airplane pilots, when countless numbers of men experience fits of aggressive behavior or moodiness concerning which they may not even be aware, let alone be able to explain.

But no matter how many opportunities open for women, there is always the possibility that large numbers of them will choose mainly to be mothers and home-makers. They may simply recoil from the competitive and stressful aspects of the world of work outside the home. It may be that the demonstrated sociability and respon-siveness of females to others will make them less compet-itive as managers, businessmen and professionals than men; if that is the case, then, to the consternation of some women's liberationists, females may not be able to com-pete in the world of work outside the home as effectively as males even when they are as or more intelligent. Per-haps the sociability of women will lead men to become less competitive, too, reducing the incidence of heart dis-ease, ulcers and suicides among them and making life generally more pleasant. It may even be that most women will continue to prefer to spend most of their middle years as mothers and to think of work outside their home as part-time or secondary.

THE REJECTION OF MOTHERHOOD

The evidence of evolutionary biology shows there can be no question that females were intended to invest a great deal of their energy in mothering. Each month the ovary sends out an egg in the menstrual cycle into the Fallopian tube, which urges the egg (if fertilized) onward to the uterus, where it is enclosed to grow an embryo and fetus. The intrauterine life which follows for nine months introduces structural and chemical changes in the body of the female to prepare her for motherhood. Then comes lactation, nursing and new hormonal changes which accompany the adjustment to infant care. The output of energy by the female for the production of the single offspring is enormous.* But in the United States there are strong cultural pressures for women not to use their bodies fully in the acts of childbirth and infant-feeding. Mothers are cut off from the event of birth through anesthesia much more widely than in any other modern nation. Compared with the Soviet Union, Great Britain and France (each of which has lower fetal and infant mortality rates than the United States), there are far fewer children delivered via natural-childbirth methods, although at the present time there is a growing interest in them. There is also a current tendency among upper-middle-class young women to re-

---

* Contrast the male. From puberty to old age, the normal male can ejaculate several times a day an average of 120 million sperm, each of which is capable of fertilizing a female egg. With that three-minute burst of energy, the male's biological fatherhood ends. It is only through culture that postnatal fatherhood was invented or can be extended—a subject to which we will turn in the next chapter.

turn to breast-feeding, but between 1946 (the last year of World War II) and 1970, the percentage of babies leaving the hospital on breast-feeding alone dropped from nearly 40 percent to well below 20 percent. Until recently, babies in crowded, short-staffed hospitals were permitted to drink their bottles alone (the bottle was held by an artificial prop).

None of this should be construed as an argument to push women who are uncomfortable with natural childbirth or breast-feeding to try either. It is to emphasize that there is an extraordinary cultural pressure in the United States for women to withhold their bodies from the expulsive acts of birth and breast-feeding, and that birthing and feeding practices in the United States tend to emphasize separateness more than in any other modern society. No one knows if babies grow into more loving responsive human beings if they were born via natural-childbirth methods or whether infants would become adults more capable of giving and receiving love if they had more experience with the smells and touch of their mothers' bodies at feeding time, but the fact is that the American preference for anesthesia and milk in a bottle have not necessarily resulted in healthier infants. For extreme contrast, one can look at the Netherlands. A vast majority of the babies are born at home in that nation, which had the third lowest infant mortality rate in the world in 1970 (the United States ranked fifteenth).

The long-term movement of American middle-class women away from natural childbirth and breast-feeding (now being reversed slightly)—however much it was related to the American emphasis on independence, separateness and privacy—did not constitute an attack on motherhood itself. In the last few years such an attack has been mounted not just in radical women's liberation journals but also in mass-circulation magazines, such as the now defunct *Look*, which ran a major editorial in 1970 questioning the pleasures as well as the significance of motherhood. More important, an increasing number of women of college age are reacting negatively to the idea of motherhood for a variety of impressive reasons. Sensing that their mothers had little influence over them and that mothers generally are losing influence over their children, watching the frustration of mothers trying to keep order among small children, realizing the grief that mothers feel when adolescents get into trouble, and believing strongly that they may have no way of avoiding the mistakes of their own mothers, young college women frequently express their apprehension about motherhood.

There are other reasons for their nervousness. Many see their own mothers as having suffocated their talents in order to be a mother to their husbands as well as to their children. They see intellectual talent which stopped developing at high school or college graduation in women who have spent their lives managing families and households in a society which says that jobs are worthwhile only to the extent that they earn money.

Traditionally, mothers could feel self-esteem in the success of their children or husbands. Now, with the ideal of independence more potent than ever, there is far less reward for many mothers in the health, happiness or achievement of their offspring or spouses. With so many unhappy children and husbands, a large number of American women are probably finding the old yardsticks extremely depressing.

To allow women to be persons they must be allowed to be mothers, too, and not to be trapped by an ideal of independence which tells them they are nothing if they are "only homemakers," or which robs the still critically important role of parenting of its significance. There are thousands of women, even in the United States, who have said that some of the happiest times of their lives came during the middle months of pregnancy, and there are others, though fewer in number, who report quite sensibly and without messianic fervor ecstatic, sensuous feelings at delivering their children without anesthesia. There are millions of mothers everywhere in the world—with infinitesimal exceptions such as the Mundugumor who detest bearing and rearing children—who experience deep joy and fulfillment in nursing and playing with and guiding their children to maturity.

To be a female who feels good as a person in America is not to deny one's femaleness. It is to control one's mind and body no less than men do, but with an awareness that female does not equal male. Clearly superior in some things, females may be inferior in others. The sexes are certainly different; and even more important, there is great variety within each sex, perhaps most of all among females, in biological and psychological predispositions.

While it is unquestionably true that discrimination against and exploitation of women has made it difficult for some of them to feel at peace with themselves, it is also true that many of the problems of being female in America come from the confusion that exists in the minds of women who believe in the ideals of independence and equality but also know that as females they are in some ways fundamentally different from males. Equality in the dignity of human personality would take into account the differences and variety within each sex, too. Mindless, slavish adherence to an ideal which denies the biological foundations of human personality may keep many women from being themselves. The end of super mother need not mean the end of satisfying mothering. To the contrary, enjoyable mothering is compatible both with stronger fathering and much wider opportunity for women to work creatively outside of the home.

IV Flight from Families

In March 1972 *Life* magazine featured its cover story on a growing phenomenon in America, "The Cop-out Mother." Without any sense of shock, *Life* told the story of a thirty-five-year-old woman, married to a loving, devoted husband and mother of three healthy, presumably happy children, who decided that her individuality was being destroyed by family life. To save it, she fled and began what was for her a creative life of independence.

The feeling of being imprisoned by family, now so commonplace among women and children, was first expressed by men in the United States in the nineteenth century. Infrequently, they left their families altogether; more often, they fled and continued to flee from family in other ways: through silence, social activities with other men and, especially, work.

It is ironic that the major complaint against the modern nuclear family has been that it stifles individualism, since it emerged precisely because of the growth of individual consciousness in men and women who did not want to be told whom to work for, where to live and whom to marry. The traditional extended family which preceded it usually was rigidly patriarchal. There was little room for what we think of as personal independence. In the Middle Ages, Western Europeans lived in enormous households of extended relationships: in addition to father and mother and children, there may have been grandparents, uncles, cousins, servants, apprentices, more distant relatives, debtors, beggars, protégés and friends. In response to vast social and economic changes (before 1750 the odds in London were three to one against a child living until the age of five), a growing number of Europeans became concerned with the transmission of property to and the education and morality of the young. But families were still extended—three generations in a household—with members locked into fixed roles and obligations. Steadily in Europe, and particularly in the United States where land was open and the families of immigrants distant, the nuclear family consisting only of father, mother and children began to reside under one roof.

With the rise of the nuclear family came the emergence of the rights of children, the growing emancipation of women, marriages based on affection, the development of a sense of individual privacy, reward for individual effort and competence and greater possibilities for significant relationships (including friendship and marriage) between persons of vastly different ethnic, class and religious backgrounds.

THE PRICE OF INDIVIDUALISM

The nuclear family did not suffocate individuality; it helped to liberate it. What was lost was a closeness to the vital events of life, a strong sense of belonging and the emotional support which several generations and large numbers of relatives gave to the individuals in traditional families.

In the extended households of the Middle Ages in France, Germany and England there was no privacy. There was much suffering from superstition, illness and death. But family relationships provided the context of education for the young. Sexing, birthing, lechering, shouting, fighting, begging and dying were an intimate part of growing up. Children could observe the boisterous traditional blessing of the marriage bed and the noisy visit by the guests to the newly married pair already in bed. There has been in the modern nuclear family a steady, inexorable "de-gutsing" of life, a cutting off from everyday, vital, intimate experience which makes young people hunger ever more desperately for it outside of the family and, ironically, also may make them more vulnerable to the inevitable pain of human existence when it comes.

The privatization of life is an aspect of psychological isolation which accompanied the rise of nuclear families; the heightened competitiveness of relationships is another. There is a sharp contrast between the familial sociability and harmony in most of the traditional extended family cultures of today and the competitive bickering that goes on in modern American families. While roles and functions are even more rigidly segregated between sexes and age groups, there is found in the traditional family an overwhelming sense of caring for (being counted on and responsible for) each other. Knowing one's place is critical. Then one knows what is expected and what is due. Invariably, place is defined by age and sex as well as relationship. At different ages, there often are different salutations, manners in eating food, dress rules and tasks to be performed, as well as different rights and privileges. There are visible signs to mark transitions from one age group to another. The major effect is to provide a sense of belonging that is missing in modern American families.

The Kikuyu of central Kenya, one of the major tribes of Africa—a nation really—provide one of many such examples of traditional family life. When a Kikuyu child is about four or five, the outer edge of his or her ears are pierced, marking a first step beyond early childhood. Then when a girl is between six and ten, and a boy between ten or twelve, the lobes of the ears are pierced by their maternal uncle, indicating that they are ready to move from childhood to girlhood and boyhood; next, boys and girls are circumcised to mark admission to full membership in the community with new roles, functions, responsibilities and rights. There is no independence. An uncircumcised male cannot have sexual intercourse with circumcised girls; he cannot have a circumcised man as an intimate friend. The tasks of the children are clear. Girls are given tiny cultivating knives or digging sticks, which, when they are five years old, they handle with amazing skill with their right hand while their left clears the soil away and gathers the weeds and grass in bundles. All tasks—girls learning how to carry babies and to put them to bed, boys learning how to milk and feed the calves—are duties to the family. There is no rejection of the family of orientation. Parents have the rights to the service of their children throughout life, since the Kikuyu believe that prosperity depends on the joint activities of all the members of the family group.

The Chinese extended family system—best known and most continuous in history—provided what may be the best example of how traditional family life with its rigid roles and patriarchal rules gave individual members both a sense of emotional support and of belonging. The teachings of Confucius, who lived five hundred years before Christ, stressed that each person must have a strong sense of his proper role in family relationships. Let father be father, and son son, he urged. But parents and children, wrote Confucius, should love one another. Particularly, children must be devoted to their parents. Filial piety (*hsiao*) was to be "the root of all virtue." For women there was little individuality as we know it. They were obliged to be respectful and obedient to their husbands and parents-in-law. Young girls were reminded constantly that to become pregnant was *yu-hsi* or "having happiness," since nothing was more important than the perpetuation of the family name. But that, plus the sense which all family members had that they were dependent on each other, gave them a strong sense of belonging.

One does not have to romanticize the Kikuyu or the Chinese—meanness and cruelty have been a part of the history of both—to see that the sense of belonging for which millions of Americans yearn was and is a part of their extended patriarchal families. The members of the Kikuyu family are together in work, joy and sorrow. When the fathers herd cattle, sheep and goats or do other jobs, the boys accompany them. In the operation of the Chinese farm, the family, men and women, old and young, all worked together as a unit, the woman's share of work being no less important than that of the man. Old men would take children to visit friends and relatives, telling legends and folk stories as they crossed the fields between houses. Kikuyu and Chinese men and women could look forward to old age. Love would not be denied them when their bodies were enfeebled and their minds faltered.

FLEEING FROM FAMILIES

How can one go it alone, be independent and yet feel the love and security that comes from continuing, dependable relationships in families? In traditional families, one shares the joy of celebrations and festivals connected with the season and rites of passage in birth, adolescence and marriage. One shares sorrows, too, of disappointment, illness and death, deepening the ties that bind. Americans want the love and security that goes with belonging but they do not want to be bound.

For some Americans the dilemma has been avoided by turning inward. Emerson provided the prescription; Henry David Thoreau, among others, followed it. Both of them saw love between persons largely as a delusion. They believed that to achieve a sense of belonging, man must change his orientation from society, including the family, to nature; only then could one liberate and understand oneself. But this was no Buddhist annihilation of self, no merging of self with nature. The self remained very much aware of its separateness. The theme recurs often in American history: society is impure; nature is clean. Whereas families limit one's freedom, the wind, sea and inanimate landscape—while sometimes awesome in power—never violate the psychological self. Nature permits and encourages the inner voice to be heard.

Thoreau, while affectionate toward his mother and sisters, lived away from home as a young bachelor until his father's death, at which time he returned to Concord to take on responsibilities as head of the family. At first he taught school. Then, living in Emerson's home, for a while he spent much of his time writing. Finally, he tried his family pencil business. But on Independence Day in 1845, when he was only twenty-eight, he put ax to prime timber beside Walden Pond and framed a hut where he lived alone for more than two years. There Thoreau, who never married or had children, found peace. There, too, this intensely shy man found a classic American answer to the problem of loneliness. Take refuge in nature and become self-reliant. "You must live within yourself and depend upon yourself . . ." he advised. But even he who believed as much as any man in the "subtle magnetism in Nature" stayed at Walden only twenty-six months. Then it was back to the pencil business with as much time as possible for walks in Concord, trips to Maine and Cape Cod and the wilderness of Canada until he died at the age of forty-five.

Millions of Americans have found inspiration and solace similar to that which Thoreau drew from living close to nature. There can be no quarrel with his observation that the mass of men lead lives of quiet desperation in their pursuit of wealth, status and so-called progress, or with his argument that solitary communion with nature often helps men and women to understand themselves better. But few Americans are capable of achieving the emotional self-sufficiency of a Thoreau. Most men and women want love. Even those who are afraid of love in families want a sense of belonging somewhere.

THE JOINERS

Unlike Thoreau, most Americans marry and begin families of their own, but they seek to make up in a multiplicity of relationships the sense of belonging which men and women in traditional societies felt in large families. More than any other people in history, Americans multiply relationships but are wary of being bound in any of them. From the late eighteenth century on, we have been a nation of joiners. "Americans," quipped humorist Will

Rogers, "will join anything but their own families." He might have added that because they reject their families, Americans are constantly looking for pseudo-families wherever they can find them. In no other society are the men's service and fraternal clubs, neighborhood street clubs, veterans' organizations, civic associations, ladies' clubs or college fraternities and sororities so important. These are social groups which are often formed to perform tasks—win games, do good works, achieve legislation—but regardless of whether they have a specific objective, there is a gratification in belonging for many of their members. Whether at a church social, garden club or meeting of the American Legion, there is the camaraderie and fellowship that comes from contact with others. The relationships are often tenuous and superficial, but because of that, they are not binding.

THE SAVING CAUSE

Evangelical revivalism has provided another way for Americans to achieve a sense of belonging outside of families. While other great religions have been family-centered, Protestantism has emphasized the individual alone in his or her relationship to God. In the camp meeting or revival hall, one may take seriously the Gospel according to Luke in which Jesus maintains that he has come to split families in order to find God. There Fundamentalist Protestants and the Jesus Freaks of today can both protect their independence and fill their craving for human contact. The Fundamentalists, more than those in high churches, emphasize the individual's lonely en-

counter with God but do it through mass singing, dancing and shouting.

Religious revivalism has swept America periodically,
from the Great Awakening in the early eighteenth century down to the contemporary outburst of street revival
meetings. There is nothing like it anywhere in the world.
To sing out together, and to share feelings of ecstasy and
hope, has released hundreds of thousands from loneliness. Even in the quieter, more formal Protestant
churches, the hymnal book makes clear that binding ties
to God (not families) are the blessed ties.

> *Blest be the tie that binds,*
> *Our hearts in Jesus love*
> *The fellowship of Christian minds*
> *Is like to that above.*

It was not so much in blood families that woes were to be
shared or burdens borne but, according to the hymn, in
religious fellowship. At the church supper and especially
at the revival meeting, one could feel the communion of
fellow-men, however fleeting.

Countless numbers of Americans achieve the same
sense of belonging through great nonreligious causes.
Salvific secular causes—whether vegetarianism or Prohi-
bition—nearly all bear the trademark of American culture. In giving oneself to an exhilarating cause it is possible to find a way of belonging and loving which shuts
out loneliness for a while, at least at the surface level.
Identification with such a cause often brings an intense
feeling of closeness to others who share the vision. It can
supersede commitment to family ties because it seems

so much more important; new brothers and sisters are acquired who do not bear the stigma of having shared the same parents.

THE NEW RELIGION: SELF-DISCOVERY AND LOVE THROUGH PSYCHOTHERAPY

Only in America are families often seen as the cause of loneliness. Elsewhere they provide relief. In traditional cultures, religion usually is very much a family matter. So, too, is psychotherapy. In ancient Hawaii, for example, when something was felt to be wrong between members of a family, all of them sat down together to talk through their problems. Although there is a slight trend toward family therapy in the United States, psychotherapy is usually supposed to take place between or among strangers.

To a considerable extent, psychotherapy has replaced religion in the twentieth century as a response to the search for salvation and belonging. The psychotherapy of and for individualism simply does not exist elsewhere. In many European countries, where only hospitalizable psychotics are treated, there is no psychotherapy for neurotics at all. But in the United States a sympathetic psychotherapist, whatever his training, orientation or techniques, can at least provide a relationship which makes the difference between discomfort and despair. Regardless of methodology, a warm, sensitive psychotherapist can give patients a sense of being cared for and of being permitted to express their hostile family feelings without danger. Complaints against father, mother, sister or brother for having done this or that to injure one's individuality make it clear that it is extremely difficult living in families where independence and equality are prized so much. Much of psychotherapy seeks to heal the wounds of separateness and competitiveness by helping the patient or client to become more self-sufficient. Thus the culture defines both the source of the problem and its cure. In a sense, self-sufficiency psychotherapy is a prescription to adjust or conform to the culture's dominant theme. The therapist asks, "How can I help my client to become more sure of himself?" Therapy often results in a clearer definition and acceptance of self on the part of the patient and not infrequently in a rejection of spouse, parent, sibling or others who are seen as interfering, controlling influences. Often, no doubt, the patient feels better for having "freed himself." But while the problem of separation has, at least for a while, been resolved, the question of belonging remains.

Those American-born psychologists and psychiatrists most influential in the field of psychotherapy, such as William James, Harry Stack Sullivan, Gardiner Murphy, and Carl Rogers—whatever their differences—all have revealed their American-ness by stressing the individual against society. Not so with the European-born psychiatrists Karen Horney, Erich Fromm, Andras Angyal and Erik Erikson, each of whose professional work developed in the United States and who saw the relationship of psychopathology to the American cult of self-sufficiency. Horney, in her book *The Neurotic Personality of Our Time*, pioneered in explaining how the cultural values of personal independence and personal achievement promoted neuroses. Each has pointed out that feelings of worthlessness can result from the extraordinary demands on the self which are made by American culture.

BASIC ENCOUNTER GROUPS: FAMILIES AWAY FROM FAMILIES

One of the most rapidly growing, singularly American phenomena of the mid-twentieth century in response to the loneliness and tensions of family life is the encounter group, sometimes called therapy group, process group, basic encounter group, workshop or sensitivity training group. The main purpose of nearly all such groups is to enhance the capacity of participants to communicate with others. An extraordinary range of groups now meet throughout the country, including prayer groups, groups in businesses and educational institutions, ex-drug-addict groups, prison groups and family groups. The appeal may be strictly utilitarian, such as getting higher profits or smoother administration, but the basic attraction which makes groups of strangers so popular is that they provide an opportunity for intense, emotional relationships without having to put up with continuing responsibilities and "controlling" influences. Where the group's members are strangers, it gives them an extraordinary opportunity to receive and give affection without the continuing obligations of a family relationship, something which America's poet laureate Walt Whitman would have understood well. He knew the terrifying side of separateness in families and sought love in intense, brief encounters which carried no implication of continuing obligation. He saw the soul as "reaching, throwing out for love," as the spider throws filament after filament, "that one at least may catch and form a link, a bridge, a connection." Whitman wanted the connection, as do so many participants in encounter groups, but not relationships which would inhibit his independence. By making all men his brothers and all women his sisters and lovers, he had no brothers, sisters or lovers. If he were living today, he would have in encounter groups at least a temporary family away from families.

Tearing off façades, removing defenses and generally de-roling oneself are a major objective of many basic encounter groups of strangers. Yet, as participants work out feelings, women and men may take on mothering and fathering roles, and both sexes are often encouraged to let infantile or childlike feelings of need and dependency rush forth. Sometimes explicit family role-playing is encouraged. Individuals describe the significant members of their families and then play-act those roles, simulating an encounter out of the past. In other groups, family history is blotted out in the effort to get close to one's present feelings. In either case, such groups can be seen as attempts to make up for the love and affection missing in dispersive American families.

Although there are an increasing number of books on encounter groups, the overall results are difficult to evaluate. At their best, such groups improve self-awareness and the ability to communicate; feelings of caring, warmth and sexuality are released. Participants may leave as more loving persons and better wives, husbands or children. Undoubtedly, the results depend very much on the quality of leadership. But basic encounter groups for strangers are peculiarly susceptible to unqualified leadership because participants are often biased against known authorities. One encounter-group leader in Boston advertised in 1971, "I am not a shrink. I am not a psychologist. I am a competent person who knows what he is doing and I am doing continuing groups." If one of the purposes of encounter groups is, as suggested in one advertisement, to "re-role yourself," there is a certain logic in having leaders be anonymous strangers, too.

Encounter groups can be coercive and even addictive. Although they are often designed explicitly to free the individual, there is in some a propensity toward a form of thought control not entirely unlike the public confessional meetings of Colonial New England congregations or Chinese thought-control groups under Communism. Here is a cruel irony! Groups which come into being because of the American drive for individual self-expression often act to stigmatize and isolate persons who are judged not to be communicating the "real me." Ironically also, in addition to cruelty, dishonesty is practiced in the name of authenticity. What could be less authentic than the person who pretends to be true to his innermost feelings all the time? But most significantly, these families of strangers away from families sometimes create a new kind of dependency, an addiction to encounter groups, which, while compensating for the loneliness and conflicts of real family life, can never provide the feelings of security and protection which blood families do. At present they constitute a massive cultural response to the dilemma of reconciling independence with a sense of belonging. Actually, they may be substituting a new kind of dependency for the old.

MAKING CONTACT: THE PERSONALS

What is most significant about the basic encounter-group movement is not that it fails to protect independence or provide a permanent answer to the need for belonging but that it exists at all. With centrifugal forces pulling families apart, Americans continue to live as what David Riesman and others have seen as a vast "lonely crowd." To overcome their loneliness, Americans have been particularly ingenious at inventing new ways of putting themselves in touch with each other.

Lonely-hearts clubs have long thrived in the United States. For decades, editors have featured advice-to-the-lovelorn columns. Now the classified advertisements of America's countless underground newspapers provide a medium for making dates, quick encounters and marriage, too. Most of the advertisements are superficial: "Highly intelligent, uninhibited, inexperienced male, 22, seeks uninhibited female to learn from." Sometimes the classifieds serve as a marriage broker: "I am intelligent, and know where I am going (law school), and need someone for a long-term relationship (marriage). She should be sensitive, and not too hip and affectionate. If you are she, maybe I can make your life worthwhile." Frequently, they refer to a previous brief encounter: "Will the girl who was in the restaurant on Tuesday at about 11:00 p.m. wearing a lavender shirt with long blond hair (sic) worn up and . . . talking to a group of freshmen please call me. I didn't have a chance to talk to you then." The dominant themes in the Personals are loneliness, emotional shallowness, cultism and a desperate reaching out. A twenty-seven-year-old boy "extends his being to a lonely female in need of love." He would be "just a friend to unload some hurts or troubles" because "I was lonely once too." A twenty-eight-year-old male assures his readers that "loneliness is a thing imagined" which can be conquered by Oriental philosophy and Eastern thought and through his helping hand and companionship. A boy who calls himself Sad Eyes writes to Dark Eyes that she may be too inhibited to love as deeply as they both desire. "I don't want to hurt you, either. You must be a truly beautiful person." Following a brief encounter with a girl from Kentucky, a boy from Rhode Island writes his "Kentucky blond" that he is lonely and helpless in trying to communicate but that he is still looking to share. Computerized dating companies take advantage of the Personals, too: "Somebody loves you; Data-Mate knows who." They provide a perfectly sensible way for lonely persons to make friends. Hardly antithetical to families, they may offer for some the only real hope they have of starting one. Yet, they are a symptom of the difficulty which lonely marriageable Americans have of making contact through friends and relatives.

In the Classifieds, one may also find advertisements for

young men and women to contact drop-in centers, hostels, hot-lines and a variety of co-ops and communes where they can get the help which apparently they cannot or will not get from their own families. Just the names of some of the places where frightened, troubled young men and women can go in the Boston area indicate their quest for a sense of belonging: Project Place, Project Trust, Project Reach and Sanctuary. Organized hot-lines are a fact of life in the youth subculture. Hundreds have sprung up around major cities throughout the country, several taking more than a thousand calls a week. They have been established in clinics, churches, community centers, hospitals, halfway houses and even in the homes of families. Money comes from donations, churches, civic groups and sometimes from state and city funds. Many youngsters would rather talk with strangers than their parents about their problems, but as important as are hot-lines, crash pads and temporary communes in providing relief from loneliness and in dealing with urgent personal troubles, they do not constitute a replacement for close, loving families whose members are committed to and dependent on each other.

NEW FORMS OF FAMILIES: THE COMMUNE MOVEMENT

Many young people now argue that the answer to loneliness in families is not through the expedients described above which do not attack the nuclear family itself. Today, at colleges and high schools throughout the country, a minority of young people are flirting with the idea of communal alternatives to nuclear families as a way of promoting both personal independence and loving relationships. Hundreds of communes have sprung up in the United States, both as a reflection of and as an antidote to the highly dispersive, mobile families from which their members come. In a great many cases, communes do not constitute communal families. They are more or less temporary way stations for persons seeking to follow Thoreau's advice to simplify their lives or at least get away from society as it is now organized.

In nearly all communes household tasks are assigned by the community through leaders or councils and there are common eating facilities. In some, property and sex are shared freely. Through such living arrangements, young communards, who sometimes are married and have children, hope that they will become both more free, loved and loving. When a commune makes provision for syste matic infant care and child-rearing by the community as a whole, it presents an alternative to typical nuclear family life in which children and parents of one biological family live under one roof. Such experiments are not new in America, and much can be learned from some which were quite successful in the nineteenth century and from many more which were not.

Successful Communes
Of the many hundreds of experiments in communal living begun in the United States, only nine have lasted

more than one generation, and the longest-lived was not
really an attempt at communal family life.* The Shakers, who at one time numbered six thousand persons in
eighteen villages, were founded as a communal society in
1787 under the leadership of Anne Lee, who preached
that she was the new incarnation of Christ, the female
half of the Godhead. Although they spoke of themselves
as a family, the Shakers were strictly celibate and enforced
separation of the sexes, each with its own governing hierarchy. No group was stronger in its attack on the biological nuclear family. All blood ties were broken and
replaced by membership in the "gospel" family. One
hymn spoke of "my fleshly kindred" as "furthest from
me." Blood relations were, in the words of the hymn,
"bad and so ugly . . . To see them and hate them increases
my zeal." By contrast, "My gospel relations are dearer to
me / Than all the flesh kindred that ever I see . . ."

Here was as explicit a rejection of the family of orientation as one could make. But the Shakers, by being celibate, were determined not to repeat that most awful of
sins, becoming parents. Calling each other brothers and
sisters, they sought the emotional warmth and sense of
belonging that has usually been associated with family
life. Combining ecstatic religion with some of the qualities of contemporary basic encounter groups, each household group of men and women held a nightly ritual in

* The Shakers (180 years), Harmony (100), Amana (90), Zoar (81),
Snowhill (70), St. Nazianze (42), Bethel and Aurora (36), Jerusalem (33) and Oneida (33).

which they danced and shook and exchanged imaginary spiritual gifts, the most important of which were hugs, kisses and exchanges of verbal affection.

There are some aspects of Shaker family life which would be appealing to many contemporary communards: their emphasis on equality between the sexes; their emotional expressiveness in the use of body movement; and possibly their rituals around spiritual fountains on magic hills populated by angels and spirits. Otherwise, the Shakers have virtually nothing to say to those who seek alternatives to the American nuclear family. In no real sense can their communities be called communal families. Sexual relations were seen as evil; children were not wanted.

Other long-lived communitarian experiments were also based on pietistic evangelical Protestantism. The Amanists, Harmonists and Zoarites, like many other communal families founded by German immigrants in the nineteenth century, drew their inspiration from German mystics and Pietists of the seventeenth century. Members of these communes believed that sex and marriage were concessions to sin. After eight years of celibacy the Zoarites in Ohio permitted marriage but continued to hold that "all intercourse of the sexes except what is necessary to the perpetuation of the species . . . [is] sinful and contrary to the order and command of God." After two generations of child-rearing, the children of the Zoarites, as one of them put it, fell into the fashions and ways of the world. At the commune in New Harmony, Indiana, which lasted one generation longer, celibacy became the rule only two years after its founding in 1805 (said the apostle Paul, "He that is unmarried careth for the things that belong to the Lord, how he may please the Lord; but he that is married careth for the things of the world, how he may please his wife").

In size, scope and strength of purpose, neither Zoar nor Harmony compared with the community at Amana, Iowa, which in many respects was the most successful attempt to establish communal family life ever tried in the United States. Begun in 1843, it lasted until 1932, when the community was reorganized into a joint stock company. At its largest, Amana had approximately twenty thousand members living in several villages in Iowa. Although they also believed that celibacy was more pleasing to God than marriage, matrimony was never absolutely forbidden. Young men were permitted to marry when they were twenty-four upon the approval of a petition to their elders. Divorce was not recognized and Amana appears to have been absolutely monogamous. Not only was marriage a concession to sin, but the birth of each child meant that the parents suffered a spiritual loss and had to deepen their piety to regain grace. Discouraging frequent contact between men and women, the two sexes ate at separate tables in the "kitchenhouse," which was built at certain intervals in each village and was usually capable of serving from fifteen to fifty persons. (At Harmony and Zoar there was no large unitary kitchen or dining room.) Men and women were segregated in their work roles, too. Women managed the kitchens and nurseries and helped with the harvests; men ran the woolen mills, flour and grist mills, printing office, brewery and other enterprises. The nurseries or kindergartens, under the command of women in each village, took children from the age of three to enable their mothers to work (at Zoar the experiment in communal child care lasted only fifteen years).

Four other of the remaining five successful nineteenth-century communal experiments—Snowhill, St. Nazianze, Bethel, Aurora and Jerusalem—also discouraged relationships between the sexes. Founded in 1800 in Pennsylvania as a branch of the Ephrata community, Snowhill preferred celibacy to marriage. Those who did marry had to seek homes outside of the cloister in which communal members lived. At Jerusalem, founded in upstate New York in 1787 by a woman who believed in her own resurrection, the group also practiced celibacy but was finished when members accepted as fact the death of its leader in 1820. Only by the loosest definition could St. Nazianze, a Catholic settlement begun in 1854, be called a communal family. While married couples were permitted to join and children were often adopted by the community, single men and women lived in separate cloisters and married couples far from both.

The Oneida Exception
The Oneida community in New York was no less committed to Jesus than the others. Like them, it believed that nothing was more important than, in the words of the Amana creed, "to live holy lives, to learn God's com-

mandments out of the Bible, to learn submission to His will and to love Him." Like the others, it was clear to the more than two hundred Oneidans that Jesus intended men and women to share property. They also believed that children should be raised in Christian fellowship. But unlike them, the Oneidans thought sex was desirable; monogamy—to say nothing of celibacy—was evil. Thus the Oneidans shared love mates and children for the sake of religious ideals for more than thirty years.

In 1848 their powerful leader, John Humphrey Noyes, moved to Oneida with a number of his converts from Putney, Vermont, where he had lost his license to preach as a minister because of his radical teachings. The essence of his creed was that believers in Christ "possessed one heart and one soul and had all things in common." The strategy was to replace the nuclear family which encouraged possessive, competitive love with one large family that shared material and spiritual lives. In Oneida, even clothes were the common property of all. As in Amana, a series of successful businesses (the most important early one was steel traps, and a later one, the famous Oneida silverware) were managed on a communal basis. Workers were assigned by a central committee to their jobs, which were rotated from year to year, and in the eyes of the community all types of work were honorable.

The distinctive feature of Oneida and its branches in Wallingford, Connecticut, and Brooklyn, New York, had to do with sex. Women wore short skirts and short hair to do men's work, and two of the principal businesses actually were superintended by women. The sexes ate, played, sang and danced together. But it was "complex marriage," a form of group marriage, that was the most unusual manifestation of the theory of equality. Noyes was determined that exclusiveness be abolished in love relations between believers in Christ. Any member might have sexual access to every other with his or her consent, and a couple could apply to live together regardless of previous attachments. If a couple became too affectionate, they would be broken up. Clearly, this was not free or promiscuous loving. Noyes and his trusted lieutenants decided who had sex with whom, when and how.

For twenty years the Oneidans refrained from having children because Noyes decided it would be a mistake until Oneida was on a sound economic footing. Birth control was practiced by having men withdraw their penises from intercourse without having ejaculated. After 1869, Noyes accepted applications from men and women to have children, keeping for himself the right to choose mates for each applicant. Of the fifty-one applications made to Noyes and a committee chosen by him, forty-two were approved. Eventually fifty-eight children were born to the community, nine of them fathered by Noyes himself.

When Noyes, this truly charismatic leader, died, the experiment in group marriage was over. The oldest children were fifteen or sixteen. They and their elders were unable or unwilling to carry the experiment further. Evidently, monogamous marriages based on romantic love were preferred by the second generation of Oneidans.

Group Marriage

Oneida is intriguing today because it presents the only example in American history of an explicit group marriage which at least raised children successfully until adolescence. In this respect, it was a fundamental attack on the two most basic and distinctive characteristics of human families—close, intense and long mother–child ties and long-term pair-bonding between the sexes. There were many parent–child relationships between various children and adults with children of their own or of others. Children did visit their biological parents once or twice a week, but they were trained to think of the community as a collective family, and the heads of the children's departments were called Papa and Mother. As was true with love between the sexes, special or exclusive love between generations was prohibited, and one child who showed a certain "stickiness" was forbidden to see his mother for a week. According to various accounts, the children appear not to have suffered unduly, but when the time came they did not choose to raise their own children collectively, as Noyes and many of their parents had hoped.

The attack on possessive love was not a total success either. It was necessary for Noyes and other elders to break up what they called "exclusive and idolatrous attachments" of two persons for each other. Young couples who wanted to be "true to each other" were punished through group criticism at basic encounter sessions which Noyes encouraged. One perceptive outside witness told of a situation in which a young man named Charles wanted to cultivate an exclusive intimacy with a woman who was about to bear his child. Quite properly, he came to Noyes for advice. The great leader listened until Charles determined for himself that his desire for exclusive love was evil. Isolating himself entirely from the woman about to mother his child, he generously let another man take his place at her side. Group pressure and the technique of public confession undoubtedly helped to enforce the ethic against intimate pairing, but the relative success of group marriage at Oneida—the community did last thirty-three years—must be attributed to the zealous commitment of its members to Christian witness and to the extraordinary leadership ability of Noyes.

A few contemporary communes are based on group marriage, hoping they can improve on the Oneida record, but the fact is that group marriage in the sense of several men being married to several women at the same time probably has never existed in any society for any length of time.* As the great anthropologist Bronislaw Malinowski explained, to have group marriage it is necessary to have group motherhood and that has been found to exist in only one small society in a state of dissolution—the Kaingang of Brazil. When others reported that group motherhood existed in Melanesia, Malinowski undertook a systematic examination of the sexual and family behavior among the Trobrianders there. He found that although the natives had no taboos against premarital sex,

---

* Group or multilateral marriages are now being tried in Denmark as well as the United States and perhaps elsewhere. The most famous group-marriage commune was led by Charles Manson.

it was necessary for a girl to become married once she became pregnant. Trobrianders decreed that children must have one mother and also one father even though they had no idea as to the physiology of fatherhood— they believed that a spirit-ancestor placed a tiny baby in the mother's body where it developed. Boys and girls were allowed to conduct a series of temporary love affairs, which led some observers to speak of group marriage. But the relationships were strictly sexual and clearly distinguished from marriage by the people themselves.

Of course, there are many societies which are polygamous, but the fact that a man has several wives does not convert his wives into group mothers, let alone make him a member of a group of fathers. The closest thing that exists to group marriage is polyandry—several men sharing one wife—and there are or have been small polyandrous societies reported in India, the Marquesas Islands, Tibet, Ceylon and Nepal. They are fascinating to study: co-husbanding among the Todas in India and the Tibetans is often fraternal; both societies practice female infanticide; the men in all these societies seem not to be jealous of each other; and they have near total power over their wives. But the main point is that no group of men is married simultaneously to a group of women who share group responsibility for motherhood except for a short time, as in Oneida, where religious commitment and leadership were unusually strong.*

---

* One powerful, ineluctable reason why group marriage may never have taken hold in human society is that maternal affection is highly individual.

Communal Failures

When Christian zeal and inspirational authoritarian leadership were missing, other nineteenth-century attempts at communal life invariably failed. The most famous of these, at New Harmony, Indiana, was led by Robert Owen, who, like Noyes, saw monogamy as a moral evil, if not a sin. How could one ask an individual to promise to love and cherish forever when human nature might produce a change of affection in a few hours? Monogamy was the cause of dishonesty, prostitution and more unhappiness than any other single institution. Since sex was pleasurable, celibacy was not the answer. How did Owen propose to regulate love between men and women at New Harmony? His plan was quite systematic. A couple desiring to live together would announce their intention publicly in a Sunday assembly. At the end of three months, if they were steadfast in their original intention, they would make a second public declaration constituting marriage. When they decided they no longer wanted to live together, they would announce their intention to divorce, live with each other for six additional months, and then split unless they had changed their minds.

Owen wanted to demonstrate that religion was not the necessary basis for a successful commune. But the experiment, which lasted only two years, was an unmitigated disaster. Every account spells chaos. The community, in the words of one of its members, was talked to death. Its one thousand members apparently had hundreds of different reasons for answering Owen's call to establish a secular utopia. Not one of New Harmony's seven constitutions could prevent the quarreling, brawling and dissension which characterized it from beginning to end.

One other famous secular commune which fared somewhat better was Brook Farm, founded in West Roxbury (now a part of Boston), Massachusetts, in 1841 and disbanded six years later. Where New Harmony welcomed drop-ins regardless of motivation, Brook Farm was exclusive. It appealed to intellectuals who rejected urban society and who believed deeply in the American myth that a simple, agrarian life produced virtue. In other ways the Brook Farmers were quite different from many open rural communes of today. Visionaries and crackpots were left out. The penniless and the ill were refused admittance. Participants relished intellectual activity, reading Dante in the original Italian, Hegel in German, Swedenborg in Latin, and the French philosopher Charles Fourier. It was Fourier's ideas that divided the Farmers and helped bring about an early demise to the commune. But a major problem was that the well-intentioned intellectuals who formed Brook Farm evidently did not know how to run a farm or a business. After two fires and a smallpox epidemic, the experiment in utopia was over.

One other commune, Fruitlands, also emerged out of the enthusiasm of transcendental philosophers in or near Boston. Although it lasted only eight months, it serves as an inspiration to some communitarians today. Bronson Alcott, its founder in 1842, sounded a call to those who wished to live a pure life in tune with nature. Ecological harmony was a major theme of Fruitlands. So was purity of the body. Coffee, tea, alcoholic drinks, pork, beef, mutton and heavy clothing were taboo. The psychological themes were also quite modern. Bronson, a follower of Emerson, asked, "Shall I teach my children the dogma inflicted on myself, under the pretense that I am transmitting truth?" The most important virtue was to be sincere, he maintained. Communitarians worked only when they felt like it. As a result, little farming or housework was accomplished.

Collective Settlements: The Bruderhauf and the Kibbutzim

Successful communes do exist today in the United States, Israel and China. But they are not group families. In every case, they are highly organized and self-sufficient collective settlements where private property is negligible. The nuclear family remains intact and parents are close to their biological children. Monogamy is highly prized.

On one of these communes in Connecticut organized by the Society of Brothers (the Bruderhauf), nuclear families live in separate houses; extensive child-care facilities are provided by the community; and—unlike most Chinese communes—kitchens are organized collectively. But, by severe contrast to Marxist China, the nuclear family, and not the state, is considered to be the foundation of morality.

The Bruderhauf was begun by a rebellious but highly religious group of young men and women in Germany under the leadership of Eberhard Arnold in the winter of 1920–21, when seven of them started a commune. In 1937 the growing Bruderhauf movement decided to emigrate to Paraguay, and from there they came in 1961 to the United States, where they now have three communities in Connecticut. This most successful of any twentieth-century American communitarian experiment is, of course, vastly different from most contemporary communes mushrooming all over the country, even though they are like the Bruderhauf in that property is held in common, child-care facilities are provided by the community and kitchens are organized collectively.

Bruderhauf life is based on piety and devotion to Christ. Arnold's theory of socialization was simplicity itself. Children have propensities for goodness and destruction. They must be guided toward goodness by loving and trusting them, but also by telling them what is right and wrong. There is no rejection of the biological family. Arnold's wife, Heini, has written that family life is of the greatest importance for every child. The Bruderhauf takes seriously the commandment "Honor thy father and thy mother." Arnold argued that a child who becomes disrespectful toward his father or mother develops deep-rooted insecurities and unhappiness which make it difficult for him to be at peace with himself. The Bruderhauf sexual ethic is also vastly different from that of most contemporary communes. Arnold warned against sexual promiscuity on several grounds: it led to untruthfulness and disloyalty; and it also tended to make one a victim of passion, thereby limiting one's freedom to make rational choices; finally, it was a crime against children since it led to instability in their lives when they might need stability very much.

Although not founded on communist principles or Christian ethics, the most celebrated and successful communes of the twentieth century, the Kibbutzim of Israel, have much in common with the Bruderhauf. Highly purposeful, organized and disciplined, they are also moralistic about sex as well as work. What makes the kibbutzim such a fascinating experiment for Americans to watch is their general method of child care. In most cases, children sleep and eat apart from parents in communal facilities of their own. Although kibbutzim may vary mainly according to their ideological orientation, children are encouraged to some degree in all of them to owe loyalty to their peer group and to the kibbutz as a whole.

Four percent of the Israeli population live on kibbutzim, many of which have seen three generations of kibbutzniks raised communally. Aside from whatever may be learned from this large experiment in communal child care, the success of the kibbutz movement must be attributed in part to reasons which are peculiar to Israel. The movement has strongly espoused the idea of a Jewish national state at a time of heightened Israeli nationalism. Many kibbutzim were set up on the borders or near the borders of hostile Arab countries to help form a defense perimeter for tiny Israel, and kibbutzniks know that the success of their settlements are vital to the survival of the nation. Indeed, far from being the haven of drop-outs or cop-outs, the kibbutz represents a national ideal for many who live outside of them.

That the kibbutzim practice socialism in property does not disturb the rest of the nation, since all leading political parties at least preach socialist philosophy. Kibbutzim marriages also accord with Israeli customs. That was not always the case. It was the original intention of the founders of the kibbutz movement to destroy the traditional marriage relationship, but that goal has been sharply reversed over the years. In the beginning the leaders shared the philosophy of Noyes, Owen and many young American communards today that monogamous marriage or exclusive love led to possessiveness and selfishness. Today, monogamy on the kibbutz is staunchly entrenched and extramarital affairs are scorned. Now husbands and wives openly and even proudly show affection toward each other despite early strictures against such "stickiness," as Noyes would have called it. Although children of both sexes sometimes share common bedrooms and even showers, as well as general eating facilities, a general atmosphere of puritanism with respect to sex prevails on the kibbutzim. While the ideologues who founded the kibbutz movement saw sexual repression in childhood and adolescence as harmful, the children of the kibbutzim ostracize boys and girls who are sexually promiscuous. A girl who becomes pregnant while still in school may be obliged to leave even if she marries the father of her child. Despite these tendencies, a few of the more radical kibbutzim still make it possible for partners who have graduated from school to share a room without legally marrying and to separate without fanfare if they desire, but if and when a woman becomes pregnant the couple must legally marry according to Israeli law, and the ancient Jewish emphasis on the sanctity of the marital

tie has reasserted itself despite the strong ideological opposition mounted against it by anti-religious kibbutzim.
As is true in China and among the Bruderhauf, wife-swap-
ping or experiments at group marriage such as those encouraged at New Harmony, Oneida and some contemporary American communes would be considered
intolerable on the kibbutz.

The Communal Alternative in America Today

The highly disciplined Bruderhauf and the kibbutzim—
to say nothing of Chinese communes—hardly provide a
model for most contemporary American communards
today, although they often seek the sense of belonging
and support provided by those successful settlements. Believing something is radically wrong with American society generally and family life specifically, they usually want
to simulate aspects of extended family life through the
sharing of household work, a widening of human contact
and experience and a sense of mutuality without the tight
and hierarchical bonds of obligation which characterized
traditional families in the past. But, as was true of the
communards of New Harmony, Brook Farm and Fruitlands, they also usually stress personal independence.

Although a minority of communes are tightly struc-
tured with a super patriarch much like Noyes, many more
of them are practically anarchic. That is the essential
problem for most of them. They repeat the fundamental
mistake of New Harmony. Communal living is simply not
compatible with everyone doing his or her own thing. A
temporary sense of belonging—an end to loneliness—can

come in a number of ways: building a building, bringing in a crop, sitting in a circle and chanting "Om," painting a mural or playing music, or through basic encounter groups. But the drive for personal independence which made so many communards flee nuclear families, to begin with, undermines collective enterprise. When anyone can drop in or out or choose to work or not to, it appears to be virtually impossible to organize work on communes for any length of time. The deep resistance to authority which underlies the formation of so many communes— the same factor which creates tension between the generations in nuclear families—eventually erodes the cohesion of the commune.

The Quest for Pseudo-Families

There are a great variety of living arrangements in contemporary communal families. In many, children remain closely tied to their biological parents. In some, children consider all of the adults in the commune as their parents. Some are monogamous; others provide for considerable sharing of sex. In a few, young mothers even boast that they do not know the fathers of their children. But most communes are not serious and systematic attempts to create alternative family systems of any kind, although members of so-called hippie communes often talk of themselves as living in a family. One group of fifty people in California called itself The Lynch Family, all members adopting Lynch, the name of the founder, as their own last name. A New Mexico commune called itself The Chosen Family. A New York City group picked simply

The Family for a name. At Fort Hill in Boston, its members speak of Mel Lyman, the founder, as the father and head of the family of brothers and sisters. The most notorious of all communes, the one led by Charles Manson in California, called itself a family.

Even in those communes which are merely havens for young runaways—more than a half million young Americans run away each year—the idea and terminology of family is often present. That came through clearly in a widely heard radio broadcast originating on station WNEW in New York in 1969 about a runaway girl named Marcy who was living in a crash pad with other young men and women whom she called her family. Marcy left her biological family because, as she put it, "I won't be owned." Later she said to her interviewer, "People won't take me as I am . . . I just want to be myself." Yet, from what Marcy said, it was clear that being herself meant being a part of a family. She confided to the interviewer that her circle of friends was a real family because they sometimes needed her badly to be a mother, and also because they let her be a baby.

The interviewer prompted Marcy to telephone her real mother and father. When she heard her mother's voice, she sobbed, "Mama, I really love you . . ." When her mother was about to put Marcy's father on the phone, the nineteen-year-old's voice shook as she explained in an aside to the radio interviewer, "My daddy never talks to me . . ." When the telephone call was over, she exclaimed in amazement that her father really did love her. Her father had never talked to her before, she commented, but now he said, "Why don't you come home?"

The answer was clear from other things that Marcy said. Home was a place where she and her sister fought, where her mother supervised and intruded constantly, and where her father never talked to her. Marcy's commune, at most, is a pseudo-family. It cannot possibly present a realistic alternative to the existing family system. At best, it can be a refuge for troubled youngsters who draw comfort from each other. In Marcy's case, it seems she was a bad judge even of her own independence. She was addicted to drugs; the young men in her "family" sometimes tied her up to frighten her for the fun of it, and she had already had an abortion.

STRENGTHENING THE FAMILY THROUGH SEXUAL FREEDOM?

Sexual promiscuity may have been a characteristic of Marcy's commune. To some extent the communal movement is a manifestation of the current American revolt against premarital chastity and strict monogamy. Premarital sex in the middle classes for both girls and boys is now common. In addition, extramarital affairs are now more widespread than ever before (perhaps as many as 60 percent of the married men and 30 percent of the women in America have had them). Within marriage there is a growing flexibility toward sexual experimentation. A small but increasing number of Americans believe that occasional wife- and husband-swapping may be a way to strengthen their marriages and their families. Where mate-swapping becomes planned and frequent it is often called "swinging." Swingers invariably remain monogamously married while attempting a series of strictly sexual relationships with different partners. In order to protect their families, some even take measures to ensure that the emotional bonds which usually go with sex do not develop (never swinging more than once or twice with the same partner). The emphasis appears to be on sexual experience for the joy of it, without emotional involvement. Its advocates argue that if swinging were possible for both partners in a marriage, possessiveness and jealousy would be diminished in the marriage relationship. Whether that is true or not, it is clear from studies already made that jealousy does exist among swingers. In fact, jealousy is a condition of human life even in those societies, such as Samoa and Tahiti, where post-nuptial sharing by both sexes is common. But the main theory of swingers is that more joyful persons will make happier marriage partners and better parents. How effectively the theory is translated into practice at this point is impossible to say, although there are a growing number of systematic studies on swinging as well as on contemporary efforts at group marriage.

While swingers speak of preserving monogamy, many of them have been married several times, although not at the same time. Thus sociologists speak of a new form of marriage, more common in America than in other Western countries, called "serial monogamy." Those who urge serial monogamy as a way of life for Americans ought to look more closely at Samoa, a well-known society where something like it already is practiced. There, when either spouse tires of the other, he or she merely goes home to his or her family and the relationship is said to "have passed away." What seems to make serial monogamy work in Samoa, apart from the readiness of extended families to care for the young, is that men and women rarely develop intense emotional attachments to each other in marriage. At an early age Samoan boys and girls are rigidly separated, and by the time a Samoan child is eight or nine years old, he or she has learned to avoid members of the opposite sex. For the next several years, boys and girls may not even sit close to each other, let alone touch each other. Then, at about thirteen or fourteen, after the onset of puberty, when it becomes apparent that the opposite sex exists for pleasure, young adolescents revel in a rich variety of sexual experience without responsibility before facing the necessity of marrying and having children. Finally, the day for marrying comes, but not for romantic love or to gain a lifelong helpmate—which the Samoans would find laughable—but only to perpetuate the prestige of one's family. Husband and wife never become passionately devoted to each other. But Americans are not Samoans. Serial monogamy—three or four or five spouses in a lifetime—as a standard practice hardly seems compatible with the desire of most Americans for intimacy in marriage.

One large modern nation, the Soviet Union, has already tried to encourage sexual permissiveness and serial monogamy. Many Soviet theoreticians predicted that a socialist society would do away with possessive mother love and exclusive sexual love between husband and wife. Their reasoning was simple. Since the child was no longer the property of the family but only of the state, the mother would feel it wrong to have possessive maternal instincts. With the modification of such instincts, she would no longer need to have the protection that comes from a continuing, monogamous relationship. To implement the theory, a program of legislation was adopted: divorce was made easy and painless; abortion was legalized; a Soviet wife did not have to follow her husband in case of a change in his residence; and a system of widespread communal infant and child care was begun. By the early 1930's the Soviet program had run into trouble. The authority of parents was undermined; children became rebellious. Many husbands left their families; rates of vagrancy, crime and delinquency among the young skyrocketed. By 1936 the 1920 laws on abortion, divorce and sexual freedom were denounced in official Soviet progaganda. Common-law marriages, which had been recognized previously in the legal code, gave way to registered marriages, which, in 1944, were given exclusive legal recognition. A nation-wide campaign was undertaken against promiscuity, bigamy and adultery; and freedom to divorce, to many Communists a highly prized accomplishment of the revolution, became extremely difficult by the mid-1940's.

The failure of the Soviet experiment in sexual freedom is not entirely relevant to the American situation. In the first place, it was stimulated by the government, not sought by the people. Since Americans appear to desire personal freedom more than anything else, it is logical that they would want to extend their independence in sexual relations as in other things. In addition, the protection which new birth control methods give against unwanted pregnancies was not available to the Russians in the twenties and early thirties. Although illegitimacy rates are rising in the United States, especially among the young, it is possible to have extramarital as well as premarital sex without pregnancy. What is relevant about the Soviet attempts at sexual permissiveness among the married is that it had a disintegrating effect on family life, a harmful effect on children already born.

Possibly the failure of sexual permissiveness in the Soviet Union and Israel can be explained by the thesis of a long-neglected but important book called *Sex and Culture*, written in 1934 by a British scholar, J.D. Unwin. The book summarizes Unwin's thorough investigation of sexual behavior in almost a hundred societies. His major conclusion is that while any civilization is free to enjoy sexual freedom, it cannot do so for more than one generation and continue to display great cultural and social energy. The cultural ascent of both simple and complex societies is closely related to the extent to which limitations are placed on sexual activity outside of the marital relationship. No civilization in the phase of ascent, such as the Soviet Union and Israel, presumes to tolerate sex outside of marriage. Since approximately four-fifths of all societies have strict rules against adultery, Unwin's conclusions are hardly startling. Even if they are right, Americans may choose (although not consciously) sexual permissiveness, as opposed to cultural and social energy. It can be argued that the values of Hawaiians, Tahitians and Samoans, with their emphasis on sharing property as well as sex, are to be preferred over the creative energy displayed by the Sumerians, Babylonians, Greeks, Romans and British at the times of their greatest splendor.

But if the analysis presented in Chapter II is correct, it is not orgiastic experience but love in human relationships which the young are seeking. Americans cannot become Tahitians even if they want to. There is no way for them to go back to the traditional extended family, including its typical patriarchal control over women and children. Nor, if this recital of the history of communal experiments is correct, can they expect long-term success in trying to establish communal families based on the ideal of personal independence.

REINVENTING THE NUCLEAR FAMILY

Despite the high American divorce rate, the growing incidence of venereal disease and illegitimacy, extramarital sex and experimentation in group sex and group marriage, most Americans still appear to remain strongly committed to the standard of monogamous marriage. In 1970 the institution of marriage was more popular for Americans than at any other time in history. Over two-thirds of all Americans over the age of fourteen were married, while in 1890, the first year for which accurate statistics were available, only half in that age group were married. More important, the latest statistics show that marriage is increasing in popularity. In 1971, the rate of weddings per capita was the highest in two decades (six out of seven divorced persons remarry). Although young people in college show an increasingly realistic skepticism about the romantic basis of effective marriage, it is clear that neither they nor other Americans have given up on marriage altogether. Rather than fantasy alternatives which seem to be even less satisfying, Americans would do better to strengthen what they already have. If the nuclear family did not exist, it would have to be invented!

What college-age Americans want from family life is not different from what most adult Americans desire: loving relationships between the sexes; affection and consideration from their offspring; opportunities to express their personalities through work, play and travel. They want friendship; yet they also want privacy. The priorities vary, of course. Some want more privacy; others emphasize work; many value intimacy and a few significant relationships above everything else. Given these goals, certain outcomes are predictable: although premarital sex will be extensively practiced and condoned in future years, most young Americans, perhaps an increasing proportion, will want their early sexual experiences to be associated with intimacy and affection; although radical experiments in group marriage and extensive extramarital sex will continue, the vast majority of Americans will prefer monogamous marriages and want them to work well; although there will be a morning-after pill which will be inexpensive and 100 percent effective, most Americans will want to have at least one or two children of their own.

Most Americans plan to marry for keeps, although they are marrying later and more cautiously than their parents did. The trend toward later marriages already has begun. After remaining stable for twenty years, the median age of marriage climbed a half year in the 1960's to 20.8 years for women and 23.1 for men. Because of effective birth control to prevent unwanted pregnancies and with increasing education, marriages will come still later. There is no guarantee that they will be wiser or more permanent, but in Sweden, where they do come later, the divorce rate is less than half of what it is in the United States (nearly 50 percent of the brides in America are still under twenty years of age, compared with 13 percent in Sweden).

The growing recognition among young people that loving involves major difficulties is a much better basis for effective family life than the typical Hollywood pap or romantic novels on which previous generations were raised. While disillusionment about marriage and life has contributed to depression among the young, they want to feel good about themselves as persons in family relationships, and although there is now a widespread fear of commitment, most young Americans can be expected to marry with the hope that they will have a satisfying, loving family life.

It only begs the question for individuals in families to ask, How can I become more independent of the others in my family? Americans who wish to feel good about themselves as members of human families would do well to take instruction from the evolutionary history of the human species. A species which has survived through learning and not by instinct can ill afford to forget its past. The distinguishing characteristics of human families—helpless children dependent on their mothers, long-term sexual bonding between adults who are dependent on each other, and a large-scale investment of energy by fathers in feeding and protecting the young—are what have made human families human.

V The Restoration of Father

In America the demise of patriarchy is apparent. There has been no comparably large civilization in which fathers have counted for so little.

THE DECLINE OF PATRIARCHY

Ignoring fathers, as suggested previously, is not an entirely new development in American history. In the child-rearing manuals of the early nineteenth century, the role of the father received little attention in contrast to the emphasis placed on the mother. Immigrants to the United States in the nineteenth and twentieth centuries were surprised by the lack of paternal power in American families. In some cases, notably the Italian, the resistance to the assault on patriarchy—at least as far as appearances go—has been considerable. But even among Italians, according to an examination of fiction, the central theme of Italo-American family life has been the breakdown of patriarchal authority under the impact of egalitarian ideals. Even in great patriarchal societies, including the Italian, the mother was often extremely powerful within the family. However, the position of the father was esteemed and extolled.

In most immigrant groups the shift in family power from male to female took place quickly as men moved out to the world of work away from home and women took on new powers in the management of a democratic household. The Irish husband and father, already hurt by poverty in Ireland, was weakened further in the United States by the demands of a highly competitive, achievement-oriented society for which neither his religion nor his Irish experience had prepared him well. The Jewish father and husband, once seen in Eastern European villages as authoritative even in silence, became, according to a rich literature on that subject, a passive member of the family, the good Jewish boy grown up. The Catholic Latin father and husband, undaunted in his machismo (a double-standard approach to sex based on male supremacy), is confused and distraught in a topsy-turvy world where women in poverty may actually be able to earn more money than men to keep the family together. Not surprisingly, it is the men who want to go back to Puerto Rico in the song called "America" in *West Side Story*, the musical play about immigrants from that island. But most do not go back. They stay because the opportunity to achieve, earn money and gain status is greater on the North American continent than back home. In making the decision to stay, they—like immigrants before them—leave the extended families of the old country to live in American nuclear families, in which each member champions his or her individualism.

Living in a society which stresses individual achievement through work, the American male has participated energetically in the undermining of his own authority as a father and a husband. Whereas political independence in the seventeenth and eighteenth centuries meant the end of hierarchical control by churches and government so familiar to Europe, personal independence of young boys and men came increasingly to mean emancipation from parental control and freedom to compete for success in the economic marketplace. It meant the liberation of talent among immigrants and the white poor, as well as higher productivity and more affluence than any society has ever known. Yet the physical and psychological cost to men specifically, and the price paid by families generally, have been enormous.

THE WEAKENED SEX

The genetic predisposition of males toward poorer health and shorter lives than females has been reinforced by the tremendous stress on competition and achievement in American life. Everywhere little boys are more prone than girls to mental retardation and to such disabilities as bed-wetting, asthma and stuttering—all conditions associated with stress. There is not enough research from other countries to show whether the differences between the sexes are disproportionately high in the United States, although there is some indication that that is the case. High they are. The figures for bed-wetters, stutterers and children with learning problems run in ratios as high as 6 and 7 to 1. With some disabilities, such as stuttering, not only are boys less likely to outgrow it, but the percentage afflicted actually increases with age.

For American males, the pressure to perform is clearly greater than for females at all ages. Studies show that small girls are permitted a wider variety of approved choices through which they can demonstrate their abilities in and out of school than are permitted to boys. Girls can play at nurse or doctor, stewardess or pilot, secretary or lawyer, housewife or businessman. In addition, girls are permitted, much more than boys, to show their dependent feelings by asking for help or by crying.

Schools are particularly hard on boys because of their emphasis on reading and writing skills which, as the evidence clearly shows, cannot be performed as well by them as girls at all ages up to adolescence. Then the pressure mounts. A national survey in 1950 showed that among children eleven to thirteen years old, 65 percent of the boys worried most about achievement, compared with 21 percent of the girls, who tended to be more anxious about personal characteristics and acceptance by others.

After adolescence come the pressures of young man-hood. For the less well-to-do, that means making good on the job, earning enough to support a family and constantly proving one's masculinity. For the upper-middle class, it means succeeding at college and then on up the ladder to graduate or professional school. In middle age the pressure may be most severe. One out of every ten American males who reach the age of forty-five will not live to be fifty-five. In Sweden, the figure would be one out of every twenty. Yet the death rate for females in the two countries in that age group is approximately the same. Even when Swedish males in that age bracket are compared with American men in the North Central United States (diet, occupation, and ethnic background are similar), the death rate of Americans is significantly higher.

In recent years, if we are to judge by mortality statistics, the pressures have become even worse. At the turn of the century the average American woman lived two years and ten months longer than the average man. Today she lives more than six years longer than he does. The men of at least seven modern countries live longer than American men. By the time an American male is forty, his life expectancy is poorer than in fifteen other nations, and at fifty his chances of living another ten years are 24 percent less than if he were an Italian (whose country is much poorer) and 55 percent less than if he were a Swede. American men seem particularly affected by diseases associated with stress. For example, five times as many men as women die of stomach and duodenal ulcers. Three times as many men as women commit suicide each year. A visitor from Mars would have to conclude that in America, for whatever reasons, it is relatively unhealthy to be a man.

THE DOWNGRADING OF FATHER

The ideal of personal independence through achievement has made American males tigers outside of the home but sharply diminished their authority within it. It is one thing to abolish patriarchy; it is another to kill father. Many Americans appear to be doing just that, according to the answers given by fifth-grade students to a question put to them in an upper-middle-class suburban school near Boston (mostly Protestant, but some Catholic and Jewish students, too) by their teacher. The question asked of the ten- and eleven-year-olds was: What does it mean to be a father? Not one of the thirteen boys and only six of the twenty-three girls had even one good thing to say about being a father. The principal theme was that fathers were tense and harried, overwhelmed by responsibility and work. One boy wrote, "You have to pay the rent, keep the family healthy, make sure that the lawn is mowed, the yard is neat." Another said, "I wouldn't want to be a father because you would have to go to work all day and spank the kids and listen to their crying and would have to listen to them talk back and you would have to help the children with their homework. And you would have to learn how to make love and that's hard."

There is not much talk of love in these responses. Surely, the zoos, circuses, parks and Little League playgrounds are crowded with loving fathers and their ten-year-old boys. Yet there is a joylessness in these descriptions. There is virtually no talk of playing together. Their overwhelming sense of father is of a man weighed down with responsibilities. There is no mention by the boys of authority, to say nothing of wisdom to accompany it. One commented, "If I was a father, I would go out as much as I could just to get out of the house. I could find something to do even if it was just to play cards with some other fathers." Then, in qualification, "I would try to stay around and have some fun with my kids but I don't think it will work."

Most of the girls saw fathering in the same terms, although a minority had positive things to say. Typical was the girl who said that being a father means ". . . making good money and getting a good job. Feeding your family. Paying the bills. Coming home to hear the problems. Going to work every morning. Coming home with a headache." Some girls volunteered that being a father was more difficult than being a mother. Said one, "I can't answer that question because a father is one thing I'll never be. But if something went wrong and I turned into a father, I'd have a bigger responsibility than a mother because I would have a family to support." Being a girl was mentioned by several as desirable. One girl said, "For one thing I will never be a father and I wouldn't want to be one. If I were a father I would like to go to work and then come home to a warm house filled with *all girl* children! [Emphasis hers.] One thing I wouldn't like is to be stuck with problems. And the man of the house usually has to face problems."

As with the boys, not a single girl spoke of the pleasure of being a father. One of them admitted that fathers do have fun but put it this way, "Being a father means going out to work every morning, coming home at night, hearing all the problems at night, all the people yelling and screaming. People asking for things. Getting headaches. Having to give food money to your wife. Paying your bills. Trying to have enough money for everything. Taxes going up. Going to meetings. Then some Saturday or Friday going out and having fun with your wife. That's the best of it."

If that's the best of it, then being the best of being a father means getting away from being a father. In all of the responses only one child, a girl, gave the classic explanation of what it means to be a father. She wrote, "It means that you would have to take on the responsibility of teaching your child right from wrong and having to set a good example for him or her. It means you would have to love and be patient with your child and not yell and hit the child but to be calm and tell him or her was wrong and maybe give a simple punishment."

But telling your children right from wrong and giving simple punishments means setting limits and enforcing them. It means exercising authority. Even in cultures where fathers do not spend nearly as much time with their children as in the United States, their authority is felt. Authority is thought to be vital not only because the child needs it but because the esteem with which the father is held by others in the extended family or community often depends on how well he exercises his authority in guiding the young. Not so in the United States. But ironically, by counting for little, father counts for much because his authority and the support that goes with it is sorely missed.

In nearly all cultures, there is a desire on the part of the young to replace the old. Some are anxious for the power and authority possessed by their fathers. They dare not judge him, at least not publicly. Rarely do they disobey him. Hardly ever do they compete with him openly. Yet the American who disobeys, judges and competes with his father apparently misses him as in no other culture. It is an American theme for a son or daughter to spend a lifetime searching for a father. Others may want to take their father's place. They may hate him. But they know what he does, what he stands for and what he asks of them.

One could write a history of the United States in terms of sons who were trying to best their fathers or, now more important, trying to find them. The adolescent son or daughter who, having missing his or her father's authority through early childhood and pre-adolescence, is not likely to have confidence in his authority at the age of fourteen. When father tries to exercise it shakily, the young feel his actions to be another invasion of the independence that the culture has so long urged them to prize.

That is because authority is the *legitimized* exercise of power in the performance of responsibility, and there are not many reasons for adolescents to see as legitimate their fathers' attempts to exercise power. Have they seen their fathers at work? Have they seen them solving problems? Do they have a sense of their fathers as respected and authoritative businessmen, teachers, master plumbers? Or do they see their fathers, as did the fifth-graders in Massachusetts, as harassed, bedeviled by bills and family problems?

What sense do children have from their American education—antihistorical and emphasizing, as does advertising, the new as better than the old—that their fathers or fathers before them have learned something which is important to them? How many fathers tell their children without embarrassment of the important crises they experienced as a child, an adolescent or a young man? What child can listen without a sense of impatience and growing intolerance of fathers who talk endlessly about the inconsequential or trivial events of youth? What child can listen with respect to fathers who preach platitudes or moral pieties and who are easily trapped in inconsistencies, hypocrisies and petty deceits? Why should children abide fathers who want to be liked more than to be respected? Why should they obey them when the pace of change and technology and consumer products makes them seem old-fashioned in style and habit? Why should they look to them for advice or help, to say nothing of authority, when their energies and attention so often seem focused elsewhere—on the job, career or promotion?

These questions reveal powerful reasons for the undermining of paternal authority. They have, paradoxically, undermined the authority of mothers, too. Super mother cannot be an effective mother. The evolutionary history of human families requires a large investment of energy by males in fathering, as already seen, and now more than ever when mother wants to compete in the world of work outside of the home.

AMERICAN PARENTS AND OTHERS

Children need loving parents who speak and act authoritatively in order to grow into healthy adults. Such parenting comes from the application of the principle of the loving, steady hand. Wake a two-day-old baby who has been asleep on his stomach. Watch his arms flail and flap out from his side until mother reaches over and applies the loving, steady hand to the infant's back. The principle of the steady hand becomes more difficult to apply in America with the passage of time. Father's hand is rarely there at all. Mother's often shakes. The undermining of parental authority by the cult of independence leads to much arm-flailing and flopping later in life. Ruth Benedict, Erik Erikson and others have pointed out the difficulties which American parents bring upon themselves by their inconsistency and, of course, the confusion which they bring to their children. Here is the greatest irony of all. Afraid to inhibit the self-reliance of their children, parents are timorous in setting and enforcing guidelines, and may actually make it more difficult for their children to grow into self-reliant adults.

In comparing parental attitudes in the Soviet Union,

Japan, France, England, Sweden and Denmark with those in the United States, the distinguishing American feature is the fear parents have of their own authority. In each of the other countries, particularly France, England, the Soviet Union and Japan, Dr. Spock would have to be thoroughly rewritten on such fundamental questions as how to teach a child to be generous, to curb aggression or to overcome timidity. The American emphasis is to permit the child to experiment. The one-and-a-half to two-year-old is likely to grab things. Dr. Spock's advice: "He is too young to have much feeling for others. Let him grab sometimes . . . it may help him to play part of the time with older children who stand up for their rights." The two-year-old doesn't like to give up his private possessions. Advice: ". . . he is behaving normally for his age. He will come around to generosity very gradually." What should a parent do when the two-year-old bangs another over the head, or at age four, plays at shooting? Advice: ". . . he is just passing through the necessary stages in the taming of his aggressive instincts. . . ." How should a mother respond when a two-year-old lets others take his toys away and push him around? Advice: "Let him learn how to get mad and stand up for his rights. It is wise for his mother not to show too much concern or sympathy, not to fight his battles for him, not to tell him he must share. . . ." The emphasis is on letting the child work things out for himself.

But the problem comes in application. Generosity does not come easily to small children; often they do not learn to control their aggressive feelings; occasionally the timid child may need a strong parental hand to assure him of support. There can be no faulting Dr. Spock for his advice to American parents. He was trying to help mothers not to be anxious as they encouraged the growing indepen- dence of their children. He was already functioning in a society where the authority of father was virtually non- existent. If he were a Frenchman, Japanese, Englishman or Russian, his child-care advice would have been quite different. The emphasis would have been on the respon- sibility of the parents to curb aggression, promote coop- eration and generally to civilize the child.

In the Soviet Union the Communist revolution at first undermined the authority of parents. That is why authori- tative child-care advice was needed. When it became clear that sexual freedom and diminished parental au- thority was leading to grave social problems, a new theory of the family was put forth under the leadership of Anton S. Makarenko, who has become at least as influential to two generations of Soviet mothers as Dr. Spock is in the United States. Makarenko responded to the uncertainty of the Russian parents who were no longer sure of their own authority. He stressed the importance of loving, but also firm parental authority. It was vital, he argued, that parents accept the authority that went with the responsi- bility of child-rearing. They should be in agreement with each other and consistent in requiring from their children the respect needed for them to become worthy contribu- tors to the Soviet state. Parents theoretically were sub- ordinated to a so-called collective family with its day-care centers, schools and children's organizations, but honor-

ing and loving one's parents became an ethical absolute
for Soviet children. Of course, these children must grow
up in a world in which there is no real intellectual, political or religious freedom; but at an early age Soviet children develop to a remarkable degree habits which Americans would see as self-reliant. To anyone who has visited
nursery schools in the Soviet Union and compared them
with those in the United States, the contrast is startling.
In place of our noisy, competitive individualism—each
child doing his own thing—the Soviet youngsters quietly
cooperate in performing the tasks at hand (dressing themselves, helping to clean, taking care of their things, finishing their job, building, gardening and cleaning up). To
the Soviet educator, the capacity to discipline oneself
comes from learning how to behave in a thoroughly co-
operative manner as part of a larger group.

The point to be learned is not that a collective family
organized by a Communist state is needed to make self-
reliant human beings. It is that children can be taught to
do things for themselves by parents or by caretakers in a
nursery through guidance rather than anarchic experimentation. There is intellectual, political and religious
freedom in Israel, France, England, Japan and Sweden.
Yet in each country, parents—particularly fathers—are
more sure of their authority than those in the United
States. In each case, love is not seen as incompatible with
the firm, steady, authoritative hand.

Swedish families appear to be considerably closer than
American families and not nearly as competitive inter-
nally. Most Swedish parents try to be aware of the feel-

ings of children and to take them into account. But parents are not frightened of their own authority. When the Swedish mother or father says, "I will spank," it is not an idle threat. Danish families tend to be democratic; children participate in family decisions. But as small children, Danes are disciplined more strongly and consistently than Americans. By the time they reach adolescence, they require less discipline.

During adolescence American children bridle at ambiguous attempts at authoritative parenting. They often see rules, even advice, as arbitrary and unfair. That they feel powerless cannot be denied. Mothers may still insist on deciding whether Coke or root beer is healthy for a twelve-year-old to drink or whether a fifteen-year-old boy may attend "R"-rated movies. While adults drink alcohol freely, adolescents are forbidden by law to smoke marijuana. From the adolescent point of view, all the adult talk about equality is so much baloney. Logically, they are correct. There is inequality in judgment and responsibility between parents and children. But many parents have failed to communicate that message consistently and effectively to their children in their pre-adolescent years.

THE RESTORATION OF FATHER

Ironically, what is done in the name of self-reliance for small children in the United States does not produce it by late adolescence or adulthood. In the absence of consistent parental authority, adolescents turn to peer groups. Research to date shows that peer-group-oriented children are less sure of themselves, less optimistic and think less of themselves than those more involved with the home. In the face of evidence to the contrary, many intelligent men and women in the United States continue to insist with A.S. Neill, the head of the famous English children's school Summerhill, that "to impose anything by authority is wrong. The child should not do anything until he comes to the opinion—his own opinion—that it should be done." It is a position no less dogmatic, if often less sophisticated, than that of the most confirmed Marxist on the virtues of the collective family fathered by Lenin. Thus paternalism has become a dirty word in America despite the need of all human beings for paternal protection and guidance. Men and women who think of themselves as loving parents cannot understand the unhappiness, disaffection and profound alienation of their children. Indeed studies show that those youngsters most deeply alienated often have loving, permissive parents, but they—especially the fathers—are seen by their children as indifferent.

The evidence is overwhelming that authoritative parenting helps produce a sense of individuality in children. Of course, the steady, firm hand must be accompanied by the quick eye, sensitive ear, open mind and generous heart. To be authoritative is not to be authoritarian or tyrannical. It is the difference between a father listening and reflecting sensitively to the feelings of his son or daughter and then communicating, "I think I know what is best in this instance, and since it is my job to decide, here is my decision," and a father asserting, "I don't care what your opinion is. The answer is no." The first reveals a sense of paternal love as well as authority; the second, merely arbitrariness.

The restoration of fathering does not mean a return to patriarchy, when the feelings of children were rarely heard, let alone accepted or indulged. The age of tyranny over women and children must end. But countless numbers of American fathers have gone to the other extreme, and as captives of the cult of independence, have loaded their children with insupportable burdens of decision-making and guilt. The restoration of fathering may mean the survival of parenting itself and the building of happier, healthier families in America.

Common sense backstops research conclusions that parental permissiveness (often perceived as indifference by children) causes confusion and low self-esteem for the young. Children constantly test boundaries, but especially as they move from infancy to childhood and early youth. Invariably they depend on their parents for help in avoiding painful mistakes. In adolescence they push against the limits of boundaries still more. Yet they still want the protection of strong, loving parents. While an authoritarian father in the United States is likely to strangle the identity of an adolescent unless he or she rebels and effectively breaks away, the overwhelmingly permissive father may make it impossible for a child to achieve a sense of himself by failing to give him or her any sense of boundaries at all.

Much has been made in the women's liberation movement—and rightly so—of the need to have husbands share more in household chores and child-rearing. They are being asked to bathe, dress and feed children and to do some of the household shopping, cleaning and cooking. But little has been said about the question of authority. Modern American families need strong fathers; but that does not mean it needs male sovereignty over females. Even if the biology of femaleness and maleness dictates that there is no perfect substitute for mother, many fathers can share more equally not just in household chores and baby-sitting but especially in supervising their children's educational and social life. How much time fathers spend with their children, what they do with that time, and whether they or their wives appear to their children as more authoritative will vary from family to family. But where is it written that it must be mother and not dad who tells Bill when to go to bed or who reminds Jack to catch the school bus? Why must it be mother who has a conference with Jane's teacher and who waits for Kathy to come home at the appointed hour? Who should tell eleven-year-old Harry to get to the dinner table on time or thirteen-year-old Sam to set the table? Who should insist to eight-year-old Richard that he is not permitted to shout obscenities or raise his fists (let alone strike) at his mother or sister? Who should speak to sixteen-year-old Harriet about the possibilities and consequences of sexual intercourse?

STRONGER FATHERS MEAN BETTER MOTHERS

What is good for children—listening, sensitive, empathic but authoritative fathers—is also good for American mothers and marriages. The desire of women for equality in sexual pleasure, education and occupational opportunities is certainly compatible with, and even may be dependent on, having their husbands play a stronger role as fathers. Spousing relationships often would be improved by a reassertion of the authority of fathers, one consequence of which would be to free wives for more active participation in the world of work outside of the home.

Mothers need help at home even if they do not choose careers outside of it, and at present they do not get much of it from their husbands. It is a fallacy to think that upper-middle-class fathers help more than lower-class men with household chores. One study showed that fathers in such families spend a daily average of fifteen to twenty minutes with their one-year-old infants and considerably less than that when the child is in early infancy. When sociologists surveyed 731 urban and suburban families in 1960, they found that the more the husbands earned, the more responsibility the wives had for seeing to it that the household chores were taken care of (although they may not have done the actual work) because the husbands were so absorbed in their careers. The picture drawn of well-to-do women constantly beset by the tasks of household management was corroborated when the fifth-graders discussed earlier were asked what they thought it meant to be a mother. Again, the responses were couched largely in negative terms, although several of the girls spoke much more warmly about mothering than they did of fathering. Mainly the talk of the boys was on the chores of mothering—buying clothes for the children, buying food and presents, cleaning the house, making the beds and diapering the babies. They saw children as irrepressible and uncontrollable. Only one boy addressed the issue of authority. He felt that most mothers are, "boss of the house because when you want to go somewhere the mother decides if you should go or not . . . the father does not know how you act during the day."

Mothers worry. According to one boy, "They worry a lot about if they [children] are all right or run over by a car or kidnapped." Another boy, apparently the younger sibling of a teenage brother, said, "Being a mother means taking a shock when your kid starts to drink . . . when he starts smoking . . . and when he has a Harley-Davidson motorcycle, you have a heart attack." One ten-year-old boy commented, "You have babies and you change their diapers, and you wash them. You give them a bath. You dress them, you undress them, then you feed them, then you clean the table, do the dishes, wash them up, set the table, vacuum, clean the room, cook, and then when you have done everything you sit down for five seconds."

The girls see the household chores, too, but many of them spoke warmly of the pleasures of mothering. It would be nice to have children and to love them, a minority said. It would make you proud to be a mother, wrote several. But the theme of worry was almost constant even for those who looked forward to being a mother. What do mothers worry about, according to the ten- and eleven-year-old girls? Just about everything. Mostly they worry about the children at school, their health and manners. One writes that the time for worrying begins at seventh grade when children get into trouble with the police, driving, drinking or taking drugs. Yet there is something good about being a mother, according to eight of the girls. Love and pride were mentioned— love for children and pride in helping them to become persons are the mother's reward.

But as we have seen, an increasing number of American women are not satisfied with the rewards of mothering. They want to be challenged by work outside of the home in order to feel happy within it. That is why upper-middle-class wives work who do not have to for financial reasons. For example, by 1970, 41 percent of the wives of professional men worked, compared with only 30 percent in 1960. Although there are some studies on the subject, it is too early to say whether such large-scale movement into the work force by women will result in maternal neglect. One thing is certain. Such neglect need not be the necessary result of occupational opportunity for women.

SUPPORT SYSTEMS BY SOCIETY

In addition to the restoration of paternal authority and better distribution of responsibility for household chores between father and mother, there are many things that can be done by society to help improve the quality of child care in the United States. With nearly six million preschool children with mothers in the labor force, there is a pressing need for child-care facilities, especially for the poor or nearly poor. With one out of every three mothers with children under six working, the middle classes need help, too.

This was the conclusion of a task force of experts who reported to the White House Conference on Children in 1970. They called for neighborhood family centers to provide a focal point for leisure, learning and problem-solving for all family members. Other recommendations asked for children and adults to come together in the world of work. Business firms were encouraged to invite children in the community to spend time at their places of work. Employees might adopt a school classroom, day-care facilities or headstart program to learn about the tasks on-the-job and perhaps to perform some of them.

The experts also agreed that preschool programs, such as those provided by headstart centers and day-care facilities, should be attached to schools and integrated into the school curriculum where they could serve as laboratories for young people and adults to learn about children and to develop care-taking skills. Related recommendations urged that curriculum be developed which would give adolescent children the opportunity to adopt a kindergarten, a day-care group or a headstart center.*

It should be possible to take advantage of the curiosity

---

* Both of these recommendations have already been combined in a course of study on "Early Child Development: A Curriculum for Adolescents," now being prepared by the Social Studies Program of Education Development Center in Cambridge, Massachusetts. Funded by the National Institutes of Health and the Office of Child Development of the Office of Education, the EDC course would provide adolescents with firsthand study and research on small children and the opportunity to help in their care.

that pre-adolescents and adolescents have about body processes, nutrition, and health and disease by giving them a major role in caring for the very young. They can learn about the human body and human behavior while they take care of children. Successful programs already have high school students teaching blind children to swim or taking care of handicapped children; they can also be used in child-care centers placed in high schools adjacent to them. Here is a practical way to help satisfy the hunger which adolescents have for knowing about human beings. It is also a way to achieve a sense of competence in something important.

Baby-sitting is not enough. That is not a real job; it is just minding the store for someone else who is really responsible. Observing and studying infants and helping them progress in the development of their minds and bodies would be excellent training for parenting and would help adolescents understand better some of the concerns and dilemmas of their own parents.

The thrust of the task force report was clear. Recommendations called for a restoration of many aspects of extended family life, recognizing that it is impossible to go back to extended families. Pre-adolescents are also fascinated by childbirth. Yet they rarely see one. Americans cannot go as far as the Hanunoo, who live in the jungles of Mindoro, one of the islands of the Philippines, and whose fathers, maternal uncles and older brothers each have special obstetrical tasks to perform at childbirth while little children watch the scene avidly. But child-care responsibilities accompanied by child-development curriculum could and should include material on the process of birth and on the development of small infants in an effort to bring Americans back into contact with at least one of life's vital events.

If these recommendations were carried through, children would have more contact with older people, the world of work and its problems. They would also have more responsibility for taking care of the young as seven- and eight-year-olds do in dozens of traditional societies where not to be asked to be a child nurse and to carry little sister or brother around would be considered a slight.

The experts went beyond asking government to act. Alarmed by the fact that children and adults spend an average of twenty-seven hours a week watching television, they urged the television industry to create an entirely new kind of television programming which no longer puts the viewer in the role of a passive bystander but which involves family members in activities with each other, in games, conversations and creative and learning activities. There is no reason why television-based curricula used in schools cannot also be shown in the evening hours at home. It is a matter of applying technology and creative resources to make programs compelling and attractive.

There are other things that American business and industry can do to support parents and help rebuild American families. According to Urie Bronfenbrenner, professor of Human Development and Family Studies at Cornell University and a leading proponent of this point of view, large business organizations can and should stop transferring personnel every few years from one city to another. They should increase the number and status of part-time positions. Leave and rest privileges should be given for maternal and child care. Flexible work schedules ought to be provided to enable employees to be with their children when they get home from school or when they are sick. Businesses should minimize out-of-town weekend and evening obligations and provide family social and recreational programs, apprentice opportunities and day-care centers.

The issue of day-care centers is increasingly important. Another task force on child care at the White House Conference, while acknowledging that little could be said about how effective fathers, relatives, friends and babysitters were in doing mother's traditional job, reported that outside arrangements, such as day-care centers, were at present unsatisfactory. In one study in New York City, 80 percent of the known and inspected day-care centers were rated as inadequate. In the country as a whole, many were found to be unlicensed, unsupervised; they were chosen by parents because they were the only available care facilities.

The need, already large, for effective day-care facilities may be staggering by the end of the 1970's when it is possible that most American preschool children will have working mothers. Yet at the time of the White House Conference report in 1971, there were only 600,400 spaces for children in licensed homes and day-care centers. Research cited by this particular task force made it clear that *properly-run* day-care centers can do much to strengthen families. Good child-care programs are expensive, but a nation that cares about its families will reorder its priorities and spend the money necessary to provide effective care for its children. That is why the White House Conference Task Force recommended a network of comprehensive, developmental child-care services at a cost of ten billion dollars to accommodate approximately 5.6 million children by 1980.

Compared with Scandinavians or Russians, American mothers have been reluctant to let children out of their care. In some respects their intuition may be sound. Research shows the importance of infant and early childhood care by mothers in the development of healthy children. But the qualities that go into such care can be distributed among fathers, siblings, other mothers, and professional staff and paraprofessionals, as demonstrated clearly over the years in Sweden, the Soviet Union and the kibbutzim of Israel. There may be no perfect substitute for mother; but there can certainly be a supplement for mother.

The provision of communal day-care facilities does not mean the end of mothering or even that most mothers will want to use them, as the experience of the Soviet Union and of the kibbutzim shows. In the Soviet Union, where nearly 80 percent of the Russian women between the ages of twenty and fifty-five hold jobs outside of their homes, it is absolutely necessary that the responsibility for raising children be shifted to a considerable extent to public institutions. But although the Soviet government has always favored communal child facilities where Communist ideals can be instilled into children, large numbers of Soviet mothers do not take advantage of them. Despite a significant recent expansion of preschools which provide complete care, only about 10 percent of the Soviet children under age two and 20 percent between ages three and seven are enrolled in nurseries or kindergartens. According to a 1969 survey, even a majority of mothers who send their children to nurseries or kindergartens say they do so only because there is no *babushka* (grandmother) or suitable neighbor to take care of them at home. Less than a quarter said they sent their children to a public kindergarten because it provided a better social upbringing than they could get at home. This in a nation where two generations of parents have been thoroughly indoctrinated with the ideal of collective child care.

Even on the celebrated kibbutzim, where parents and children usually do not share common living quarters, parents, and especially mothers, have developed more intimate and intense relationships with their children than the early ideologues of the movement had thought desirable. Nearly all kibbutzim mothers nurse their infants until nine months, and almost every parent has a special time—as long as two or three hours—during the day with his or her natural children. Even so, some women complain that they do not have enough time with their children; they especially want to be with them at night when they go to sleep and in the morning when they wake up. As a consequence, twenty-six of Israel's two hundred and fifty kibbutzim have begun to shift responsibility for mothering back to the mother by building more rooms onto an individual family's house or apartment and sending the children home at 4 P.M. to spend the night. The explanation given by women for the return to mothering adds up to a reaffirmation of *Homo sapiens'* evolutionary history. They want more intense, intimate and continuing responsibility for the care of their children. When a mother is unhappy with a nursemaid on a kibbutz, she may stay home to take care of her own child even though she has heard strictures against doing so one hundred times or more. Once women are given the opportunity to share child-care responsibility with others, they are then free to choose not to.

None of this is to say that the system of communal child care either in the Soviet Union or on the kibbutzim is not working. It only points out that maternal feelings remain powerful in the face of ideological opposition. The human mother invests too much energy in the protection of her offspring not to want to maintain a very special relationship with them, except in unusual cases. In such instances the result may be seriously harmful to children. Research on maternal deprivation shows that neglected children cannot develop into healthy adults except in the most rare cases. Without warm, loving affection from a mother or a substitute, such as a father, grandmother, relative, neighbor or nurse, the human infant will be crippled beyond repair. Thus it is not only necessary to build day-care centers; they must be very good.

There is a justified desire on the part of women to be

freed from the burdens of household chores, to have fathers become more responsible for their children, and to have genuine opportunities to apply their minds outside of the home. When all this takes place, it is entirely possible that, as has already happened on the kibbutz, many women will choose to spend more time mothering. Equality between the sexes was and remains a central kibbutzim ideal. It meant and still means that women should not be limited to child-rearing and homemaking but should have an opportunity to do other kinds of worthwhile work. Yet, with the passage of time on nearly all kibbutzim, women have become specialists in cooking, sewing, laundry work, nursing or child care rather than, as in the United States, generalists who, in the traditional routine of housekeeping and mothering, do a variety of things in the course of a day. Some women on the kibbutz have complained about the return of traditional work roles, but few have protested against nursing their own infants or the growing tendency to have more contact with their own children. Fathers can help mothers, and older siblings, too; and so can day-care centers. Then mothers may become more relaxed about mothering. As opportunities open for them in the world of work outside of the home, many may feel more comfortable when they remain in it. There are even many jobs where mothers can bring their small children—even infants who are still nursing—to work with them, drop them off at the nursery and be available for feeding or emergencies. Businesses, social service agencies, governmental buildings, schools and manufacturing plants should be planned in such a way that mothers can stay close to their infants and small children without having to shut themselves off from interesting work and contact with others. Plans for residential areas can include facilities for communal cooking and laundry (as well as basketball courts and swimming pools) so that women and men may, if they choose, rotate in the management of certain household responsibilities.

Government policy should subsidize the building of apartment complexes for the aged in existing and new residential communities in order to help bring grandparents and small children back into each other's lives. Such moves would not help mother; they would strengthen all members of the family who need a sense of belonging in communities as well as in families. It is probably impossible to slow down the rate with which men change jobs in the United States and with which families move their place of residence (in the last decade, one-half of all families moved every five years), but much can be done to bring families closer together for mutual support and to make it possible for them to become part of a community soon after they arrive.

When De Tocqueville wrote about the psychological isolation of Americans in the 1840's, he pointed to what would continue to be the central American problem in human relations. But he was writing about a rural America in which populations were relatively stable compared with what they are now. It was far from an idyllic time—there was vicious prejudice against outsiders and meanness within families, too. But there were church suppers, village fairs, spelling bees and July Fourth celebrations where three generations of a single family felt with other family groups that they belonged to a community.

Ever since De Tocqueville wrote, and before, those communities have been broken up as young men and women left them (and still do) for economic opportunity, intellectual stimulation, entertainment and excitement in cities and suburbs. It is impossible to re-create the rural communities of America's past, even if one wanted to; but it is not impossible to do something about strengthening family and community in America's cities and suburbs.

The essential problem is attitude. As long as Americans value above everything else personal independence, with its emphasis on privacy and fear of commitment, families will be in serious trouble and communities virtually non-existent.

IN PRAISE OF DEPENDENCE

The American assumption has been that what promotes independence is good for individuals. One can say of the wreckage found in American families today that the cure lies in some new arrangement based on more independence. That would be a classic American prescription. But the prescription, far from being therapeutic, is itself a major cause of discomfort. There is no need to go back to the stifling, rigidly controlled patriarchal families of old. The exploitation of women by men should be buried along with the dodo bird and the dinosaur. There is no possible excuse for the brutalization of children through the unthinking, insensitive and arbitrary domination of them. But human beings need each other in close, continuing relationships at all ages of their lives. That is the central meaning of the evolutionary history of human families. Infants are helpless and need close, intimate mothering; children need fathers long after the biological mission of adult males is finished; and men and women need each other in dependable relationships which grow out of commitment and will, not instinct or loneliness.

Families which begin with love marriages have enough difficulty without being burdened by mindless assumptions about independence. There is bound to be attrition of some of the factors which promoted marriage in the first place. The spontaneity and mystery of romance before marriage are replaced by routine and familiarity. Differences in personality which may have seemed attractive at first—optimist versus pessimist, verbal versus nonverbal, extrovert versus introvert—make good communication difficult over the years. People change in different ways during several decades of marriage. There are reasons enough to grow apart.

But the central reason in America for families flying apart lies in the competition and conflict caused by the culture's emphasis on personal independence through achievement. Husbands exercise it in the world of work; children assert it at home; wives hunger for it in their private worlds. To overcome their isolation from each other, they must begin to question the cult of independence which makes authority and dependency bad words at home and promotes fierce competition for achievement outside of it. In this respect, the assault of the young on productivity values—with all of its excesses—may be extremely helpful. The decline of competitive achievement may reduce the nation's gross national product, but it may also allow for more loving. But many of the young seem loath to acknowledge that human loving has to do with reciprocity of responsibility, obligation and dependency, as well as knowing when to let others alone. Human love in any relationship requires a different mix of interfering and noninterfering love. The art of loving consists in knowing when and how to interfere. Because in the United States there is such a strong cultural bias against interference—don't tread on me and don't violate the independence of the other—the response to interfering love is frequently an angry one.

That is why it is extremely important for spouses to listen to each other—to hear feelings as well as words—and to understand that the impulse to interfere may be motivated by a deep sense of commitment to the welfare and growth of the other, not the neurotic need to dominate. Listening with compassion is extremely difficult. Yet compassion is needed to overcome the arrogance and self-righteousness that accompany the cult of individualism. Parents who rigidly embrace the shibboleths of the past out of a neurotic fear of change cannot hear the young; children who shout mindless slogans of change terrify the old. Women who breathe hot fire against the oppression of men, and men who fight back with vitriolic retorts or who run away, have produced a chain reaction of hostility that can be broken only by compassion. From compassion may come understanding. With understanding, perhaps wisdom. It is wisdom which is needed to live the good life, not a humanity-stifling devotion to the cult of the individual.

The title of a popular song in the 1970's, "I've Got to Be Me," revealed once again the American fear of society. Whenever I heard it I felt like shouting into the radio: "Of course, you've got to be you. Who else are you? What are you afraid of? How can you become you without loving and being loved by others?" There is no individual without society. When will Americans learn that? There is no group in society more capable of nurturing the creative, loving spirit of human beings than the family. To flee from family is to abandon humanness.

Notes

CHAPTER I: THE AMERICAN-NESS OF IT ALL

The Family under Attack

The Watson quotation and other citations from behaviorists in the nineteen-twenties and thirties come from a small volume edited by Ashley Montagu, *Marriage: Past and Present* (Boston: Porter Sargent, 1956), and were cited by the great anthropologist Bronislaw Malinowski. David Cooper's *The Death of the Family* (New York: Pantheon, 1970) is a comprehensive if somewhat unintelligible attack on the family and bourgeois capitalist society. It joins psychological theories to older Marxist critiques. See Karl Marx, "Family Life Under the Factory System," in *Das Kapital* (New York: Modern Library, 1906); see also Friedrich Engels, *The Origin of the Family, Private Property and the State* (New York: International Publishers, 1942).

Along with these systematic attacks have come many popular critiques in the mass media such as "The American Family: Future Uncertain," *Time* (December 28, 1970); "Motherhood: Who needs It?" *Look* (September 22, 1970), by Betty Rollin; and "Is the Family Obsolete?," *Look* (January 26, 1971). Many of the critiques have come from sociologists: see Richard Sennett's "Breakup of the Family," *The New York Times* (July 19, 1971); and Leo David's "Tomorrow's Marriage Styles," *Current* (January 1972). More have come from the women's liberation movement. Germaine Greer's *The Female Eunuch* (New York: McGraw-Hill, 1970) contains a strong attack on the family. Linda Gordon's *Families* (Boston: Bread and Roses Publication, 1970) calls for the destruction of families as we know them. A powerful indictment comes in a book by Shulamith Firestone, *The Dialectic of Sex: The Case for Feminist Revolution* (New York: Bantam, 1971). Two recent textbooks which offer compilations of articles criticizing the modern nuclear family or suggesting alternatives are: Herbert A. Otto (ed.), *The Family in Search of a Future* (New York: Appleton-Century-Crofts, 1970); and Arlene S. Skolnick and Jerome Skolnick *The Family In Transition: Rethinking Marriage, Sexuality, Child Rearing and Family Organization* (Boston: Little, Brown, 1971).

Evolution and Ethology

I am indebted to many students of evolution and to the work of primate ethologists. The theory of the evolution of human families presented here leans on the work by John E. Pfeiffer,

David Pilbeam, L.S.B. Leakey, Weston La Barre, W. E. Le Gros Clark, Ashley Montagu, and Theodosius Dobzhansky. See Pfeiffer, *The Emergence of Man* (New York: Harper & Row, 1969); Pilbeam, *The Evolution of Man* (New York: Funk & Wagnalls, 1970); Leakey, *Adam's Ancestors: The Evolution of Man and His Culture* (New York: Harper & Row, 1960); La Barre, *The Human Animal* (Chicago: The University of Chicago Press, 1954); W. E. Le Gros Clark, *The Antecedents of Man* (New York: Harper & Row, 1963); Dobzhansky, *Mankind Evolving: The Evolution of the Human Species* (New Haven, Conn.: Yale University Press, 1962); Montagu, *Man: His First Two Million Years* (New York: Delta, 1970). For the reader who is limited to one book, I would choose Pfeiffer, since his volume thoroughly incorporates recent discoveries in archeology and primate behavior.

Other useful volumes which get at fundamental issues in the relationship of biology to culture and which bear upon the theory of the evolution of human families presented include: George Gaylord Simpson, *Biology and Man* (New York: Harcourt, Brace & World, 1964); Lesley A. White, *The Evolution of Culture* (New York: McGraw-Hill, 1965), Chapter IV ("The Transition from Anthropoid Society to Human Society"); E. D. Chapple, *Culture and Biological Man* (New York: Harcourt, Brace and Jovanovich, 1970); and particularly Irenäus Eibl-Eibesfeldt, *Ethology: The Biology of Behavior* (New York: Harcourt, Brace & Jovanovich, 1970), an excellent comparative study of behavior.

In making comparisons between the other primates and humans, I relied heavily on Irven De Vore (ed.), *Primate Behavior: Field Studies of Monkeys and Apes* (New York: Holt, Rinehart & Winston, 1965). Another volume edited by De Vore and Richard B. Lee, *Man the Hunter* (Chicago: Aldine, 1968), is also extremely good. Superbly organized and illustrated is *The Life of Primates* (New York: Universe Books, 1969), by Adolph H. Schultz. For an excellent series of essays on the socio-sexual behavior of apes and monkeys, see Desmond Morris (ed.), *Primate Ethology* (Garden City, N.Y.: Anchor Books, 1969). I have been particularly influenced by the work of De Vore on baboons and through it by the work of Jane Van Lawick-Goodall on chimpanzees, George B. Schaller on gorillas and J. O. Ellefson on gibbons. See, for example, De Vore, "Mother-Infant Relations in Free Ranging Baboons," in Harriet L. Rheingold (ed.), *Maternal Behavior in Mammals* (New York: John Wiley & Sons, 1963); Van Lawick-Goodall, "The Behavior of Free-Living Chimpanzees in the Gombe Stream Reserve," *Animal Behavior Monographs* (1:3, 1968); Schaller, *The Year of the Gorilla* (New York: Ballantine, 1964); and an unpublished article by Ellefson entitled "A Natural History of Gibbons in the Malayan Peninsula."

Also through De Vore my attention was brought to the work of Robert Trivers. See particularly an unusually provocative article, "Parental Investment and Sexual Selection," in *Sexual Selection and the Descent of Man, 1871–1971* (Chicago: Aldine-Atherton, 1972), edited by B. Campbell.

The work of ethologists Konrad Lorenz and Desmond Morris has also been stimulating and helpful. See Lorenz, *On Aggression* (New York: Harcourt, Brace & World, 1966); and Morris, *The Naked Ape* (New York: Dell, 1967) and *The Human Zoo* (New York: Dell, 1969). Somewhat more speculative but certainly suggestive are dramatist-writer Robert Ardrey's *African Genesis* (New York: Atheneum, 1961) and *The Territorial Imperative* (New York: Atheneum, 1966), and anthropologist Lionel Tiger's *Men in Groups* (New York: Random House, 1969).

What these writers have in common is the belief that man is an animal among other animals and that one can learn much about the nature of human beings from studying other animals, a view which seems persuasive to me, though I would not deny for a moment that man is also fundamentally different from other animals.

Also on the origins of the family and specifically on the issue of matriarchy and patriarchy, see Kathleen Gough, "The Origin of the Family," *Journal of Marriage and the Family* (November 1971). Dr. Gough, an anthropologist and strong proponent of women's rights, concedes that the evidence supports the view that women have from the beginning been subordinated to men in families. That is not the view held by others who write for the women's liberation movement. They refer often to two speculations concerning matriarchy that have been discredited despite their ingenuity. See J. J. Bachofen's *Das Mutterrecht* (Basel: B. Schwab, 1897), hypothesizing on the basis of scholarly analysis of the mythologies of the Near East that matriarchies preceded patriarchies; and the more famous *The Mothers*, by Robert Briffault, first published in 1927 and now available through Universal Library (New York, 1953). Great controversy developed around Briffault's work, an impressive speculation with an even more impressive marshaling of facts to support it; but partly through the critiques of Bronislaw Malinowski and others, the established view is the one reported by Gough.

History of American Families

Every writer of social history is obligated to a superb social history of family life in Europe by Philippe Ariès, *Centuries of Childhood* (New York: Vintage Books, 1962), which essentially traces the history of childhood from the Middle Ages until modern times in France. Earlier books on the United States which have been helpful include Charles M. Andrews, *Colonial Folkways: A Chronical of American Life in the Reign of the Georges* (New Haven, Conn.: Yale University Press, 1919); Alice M. Earle, *Childlife in Colonial*

Days (New York: Macmillan, 1899), and by the same author, *Colonial Dames and Good Wives* (Boston: Houghton Mifflin, 1895); and mainly, Arthur W. Calhoun's *A Social History of the American Family* (New York: Barnes & Noble, 1945) in three volumes. Calhoun's work is the only attempt at a large history of the American family. While it contains a great deal of information it is almost totally lacking in analysis. Nonetheless, my debt to Calhoun is considerable. I drew on many references in his thorough bibliography to check firsthand some of the quotations and anecdotes told in his book. Somewhat different but helpful approaches to the study of American family life may be found in Max Lerner's *America as a Civilization* (New York: Simon and Schuster, 1957), Part A, "Life Cycle of the American"; and John Sirjamaki's *The American Family in the Twentieth Century* (Cambridge, Mass.: Harvard University Press, 1953). Colonial historian Edmund S. Morgan has provided two superb studies of family life in the seventeenth and eighteenth centuries: *The Puritan Family: Religion and Domestic Relations in Seventeenth-Century New England* (New York: Harper), revised and enlarged in 1966; and *Virginians at Home: Family Life in the Eighteenth Century* (Charlottesville, Va.: Dominion Books), reprinted in 1968. Also see John Demos's *A Little Commonwealth: Family Life in Plymouth Colony* (New York: Oxford University Press, 1970), a jewel of a book.

There are two thoughtful unpublished (to my knowledge) papers, both by distinguished historians, which should be read by anyone trying to write on the history of the American family. These are Edward M. Saveth, "The Problem of American Family History," written in 1968; and William R. Taylor, "Domesticity in England and America, 1770–1840," written in 1964.

There are a number of excellent journal articles contributing to an understanding of the history of the American family.

Important for me were Phillip J. Greven, Jr., "Family Structure in 17th-Century Andover, Massachusetts," *William and Mary Quarterly* (April 1966); and by the same author, "Historical Demography and Colonial America," *William and Mary Quarterly* (July 1967). Much of the journal work is in the area of demography. For recent examples, see John Mondell, "Family and Fertility on the Indiana Frontier, 1870," *American Quarterly* (December 1961), or an article by Susan E. Bloomberg, Mary Frank Fox, Robert M. Warner and Sam Bass Warner, Jr., "A Census Probe into 19th-Century Family History: Southern Michigan 1850–1880," *Journal of Social History* (Fall 1971). As the authors of the latter article point out, the most systematic information about the American family comes from historians of social mobility such as Stephan Thernstrom, *Poverty and Progress, Social Mobility in the Nineteenth-Century City* (Cambridge, Mass.: Harvard University Press, 1964). Also helpful to me were sociologist Richard Sennett's *Families Against the City: Middle-Class Homes of Industrial Chicago, 1872–1890* (Cambridge, Mass.: Harvard University Press, 1970) and two other historical works on New England towns: Sumner Chilton Powell's *Puritan Village* (Middletown, Conn.: Wesleyan University Press, 1963) and Kenneth A. Lockridge's *A New England Town, The First Hundred Years: Dedham, Massachusetts, 1636–1736* (N.Y.: W. W. Norton, 1970).

Through all of these works I learned much about the dispersiveness within and mobility of American families throughout American history. But it is Calhoun, who relies so heavily on the observations of foreign visitors as well as on a wealth of popular articles in newspapers and magazines and books, to whom I am most indebted. Because of him, I read much further into the accounts of foreign visitors and immigrants who provided a comparative perspective in looking at the American family as a system. Thus I have frequently quoted foreign observers on the American family. Only in the case of

Alexis de Tocqueville have I cited the source. De Tocqueville's famous two-volume *Democracy in America*, published in many editions, remains the outstanding interpretation of the American character. There is no one on whom I have drawn more heavily, although he and I are at variance on certain key points. Writing in the 1830's, De Tocqueville did not see American adolescence as a particularly troubling time. Nor was he impressed by the assertiveness and power of American married women. Indeed, it was his tendency not to see conflict in the American family or conflict in America at all, except among Indians, whites and blacks. The fact is that adolescence was not as drawn out and not nearly as troublesome in the early nineteenth century as it became a hundred years later. Also, American middle-class women were more domestically inclined and loyal to their husbands than many aristocratic women he knew in France. But even during the time of De Tocqueville's observations, other foreign visitors were impressed by the assertiveness of American married women and American youth.

For excellent compilations of foreign observations plus appropriate bibliographies, see *This Was America: As Recorded by European Travelers in the Eighteenth, Nineteenth, and Twentieth Centuries* (New York: Harper and Row, 1949), edited by Oscar Handlin; and *America in Perspective* (New York: Random House, 1947), edited by Henry Steele Commager.

The American Family as a System

Comments of foreigners were helpful in understanding the distinctiveness of the American family system. Ethnographic studies were also important. A truly monumental book on the family is Carle Zimmerman's *Family and Civilization* (New York: Harper & Bros., 1947). Zimmerman may have been the first to see American families as particularly atomistic. An excellent quick survey on various kinds of family systems appears in *The Family in Various Cultures*, 3rd ed. (Philadelphia: J. B. Lippincott, 1967), Stuart A. Queen and Robert W. Habenstein. Another excellent survey, even more comprehensive and rich in data although less readable, is *The Family in Cross-Cultural Perspective* by William N. Stephens (New York: Holt, Reinhart & Winston, 1963). Two tremendously important comparative studies which are worth reading from beginning to end are William J. Goode's *World Revolution and Family Patterns* (Glencoe, Ill.: Free Press, 1963) and *Marriage, Family and Residence* (New York: The Natural History Press, 1968), edited by Paul Bohannan and John Middleton. The last has the disadvantage of being a collection of articles, but it is a superb collection which helps one to think in terms of systems. Finally, there is George P. Murdock, *Social Structure* (New York: Macmillan, 1949), which provides a wealth of information on comparative family systems.

American Values

In addition to De Tocqueville's great work, there are several significant studies of American values and character by Americans to which my work owes much. Included are David Riesman's *The Lonely Crowd* (New Haven, Conn.: Yale University Press, 1950); Seymour Lipset's *The First New Nation* (New York: Basic Books, 1963); R. W. B. Lewis' *The American Adam* (Chicago: University of Chicago Press, 1955); and Leon Howard's *Literature and the American Tradition* (Garden City, N.Y.: Doubleday, 1960). The interpretation of American literature as a way of illuminating the American character has a long tradition in American studies. Two recent volumes which backstop many of my own interpretations are Quentin Anderson's *The Imperial Self: An Essay in American Literary and Cultural History* (New York:

Alfred A. Knopf, 1971) and William E. Bridges' *Three Spokesman for the Self: Emerson, Thoreau and Whitman* (Scranton, Pa.: Chandler, 1971). I have long been indebted to Professor Bridges for having shown me his unpublished Ph.D. thesis on "The Family Circle in American Verse: The Rise and Fall of an Image" (1963) and the excellent article on which it is based, "Family Patterns and Social Values in America, 1825–1875," in *The American Culture: Approaches to the Study of the United States* (Boston: Houghton Mifflin, 1968), edited by Hennig Cohen. Bridges helped me to understand Emerson, although not as sympathetically as he does. For a more complete review of Emerson, see Alfred Kazin and Daniel Aaron (eds.), *Emerson: A Modern Anthology* (New York: Houghton Mifflin, 1958). My own interpretation of American values and character appears in *Those Peculiar Americans* (New York: Meredith Press, 1967).

In this chapter, I make it clear that it is about middle-class families that I am writing—those families in which the head of the household has a professional, management or white-collar occupation, and which are grouped in the upper-middle class of the prestige-income ladder, and those families whose aspirations are similar to those in the upper-middle class. For those who wish to read about families of the less well-to-do, see Mirra Komarovsky, *Blue-Collar Marriage* (New York: Random House, 1964); Lee Rainwater, Richard P. Coleman and Gerald Handel, *Workingman's Wife: Her Personality, World and Life Style* (New York: McFadden, 1962); and Andrew Billingsley, *Black Families in White America* (Englewood Cliffs, N.J.: Prentice-Hall, 1968); Jessie Bernard, *Marriage and Family Among Negroes* (Englewood Cliffs, N.J.: Prentice-Hall, 1966); Eliot Liebow, *Tally's Corner* (Boston: Little, Brown, 1966); and Lee Rainwater, "Crucible of Identity: The Negro Lower-Class Family," *Daedalus* (Winter 1966).

Chapter II: In the Kingdom of the Young

Small Children

In addition to Calhoun, Earle, the historical monographs
cited above, and the observations of foreign visitors, the following were extremely useful: Robert H. Bremner et al.
(eds.), *Children and Youth in America: A Documentary History*, Vol. 1, 1600–1865 (Cambridge, Mass.: Harvard University Press, 1970), a magnificent source book of more than
eight hundred pages of documents and bibliography; Richard
L. Robson, "The American Child as Seen by British Travelers,
1845–1935," *American Quarterly* (Fall 1965); Robert Sunley,
"Early Nineteenth-Century Literature on Child-Rearing," in
Margaret Mead and Martha Wolfenstein (eds.), *Childhood
in Contemporary Cultures* (Chicago: University of Chicago
Press, 1963); Richard D. Mosier, *Making the American Mind:
Social and Moral Ideas in the McGuffey Readers* (New York:
King's Crown Press, 1947); Daniel R. Miller and Guy Swan-
son, *The Changing American Parent: A Study in the Detroit
Area* (New York: John Wiley & Sons, 1958); Horace E.
Scudder, *Childhood in Literature and Art* (Boston: Hough-
ton Mifflin, 1900); Martha Wolfenstein, "Fun Morality: An
Analysis of Recent American Child Training Literature,"
Journal of Social Issues (7:4, 1951); Françoise Dolto, "French
and American Children as Seen by a French Child Analyst,"
translated by Nathan Leites, in *Mead and Wolfenstein, op.
cit.* For a recent article which sums up sociological literature
on sibling rivalry, see Donald P. Irish, "Sibling Interaction:
A Neglected Aspect in Family Life Research," *Social Forces*
(42) 1964; for contemporary studies on American child-
rearing, see Robert S. Sears, Eleanor Maccoby, and Harry
Levin, *Patterns of Child Rearing* (Evanston, Ill.: Row, Peterson & Co., 1957); John L. Fischer and Ann Fischer, *The New*

Englanders of Orchardtown, U.S.A. (New York: John Wiley & Sons, 1966); and for the great child-care manual of our time, see Benjamin Spock, *Baby and Child Care*, 1st ed. (New York: Pocket Books, 1946).

Adolescence

Very helpful is the work of Erik H. Erikson, especially his *Childhood and Society* (New York: W. W. Norton, 1950) and "Identity and the Life Cycle," in *Psychological Issues* (New York: International Universities Press, 1959). A solid psychoanalytic interpretation is Peter Blos's, *On Adolescence: A Psychoanalytical Interpretation* (New York: The Free Press, 1961). For firsthand accounts of the feelings and ideals of adolescents from all over the world, see Norman Kiell, *The Universal Experience of Adolescence* (New York: International Universities Press, 1963). A more useful collection of statements by American youth is *Experiencing Youth: First-Person Accounts*, by George W. Goethals and Dennis S. Klos (Boston: Little, Brown, 1970). An excellent sociological perspective can be found in A. B. Hollingshead, *Elmstown Youth* (New York: John Wiley & Sons, 1959). A well-written analysis of American teenagers is Grace and Fred M. Hechinger's *Teen-age Tyranny* (New York: William Morrow, 1963). For cross-cultural perspectives, the following are rewarding: Ruth Benedict, *Patterns of Culture* (Boston: Houghton Mifflin, 1934); Margaret Mead, *Coming of Age In Samoa* (New York: Dell, 1968); Lawrence Wylie, *Village in the Vaucluse* (New York: Harper & Row, 1957); Margaret Mead, "Adolescence in Primitive and Modern Society," in Eleanor Maccoby, Theodore Newcomb, and Eugene Hartly (eds.) *Readings in Social Psychology* (New York: Henry Holt, 1958); and John W. Whiting, C. Kluckhohn, and A. Anthony, "The Function of Male Initiation Ceremonies at Puberty" in the same volume.

Certain articles on parent–youth conflict have become classics over the years. Two of the most important are Kingsley Davis, "The Sociology of Parent–Youth Conflict," *American Sociological Review* (5), 1940; and Ruth Benedict, "Continuities and Discontinuities in Cultural Conditioning," in Martin Stendler (ed.), *Readings in Child Development* (New York: Harcourt, Brace, 1954).

On the question as to whether there is an adolescent culture at all, two excellent articles take a negative view: Bennet Berger, "Adolescence and Beyond," *Social Problems* (10), 1963; and Frederick Elkin and William J. Westley, "The Myth of the Adolescent Peer Culture," *American Sociological Review* (20), 1955. But there is a good deal written on the other side. See James S. Coleman, *The Adolescent Society* (New York: The Free Press, 1961). Probably the most sensitive interpreter of upper-middle-class young men and women is Kenneth Keniston; see *The Uncommitted* (New York: Harcourt, Brace & World, 1960) and *Young Radicals* (New York: Harcourt, Brace & World, 1968). Other interpretations popular with the young themselves are Theodore Roszak, *The Making of a Counter-Culture: Reflections on the Technocratic Society and Its Youthful Opposition* (New York: Doubleday, 1969); and Paul Goodman, *Growing up Absurd* (New York: Random House, 1960), which is mainly about boys growing up; and a recent bible of the counter-culture, Charles A. Reich, *The Greening of America* (New York: Random House, 1970).

Other useful attempts to interpret teenage culture include John Barron Mays, *The Young Pretenders: Teenage Culture in Contemporary Society* (New York: Schocken, 1965); and at a less analytical but more descriptive level, J. I. Simmons and Barry Winograd, *It's Happening: A Portrait of the Youth Scene Today* (Santa Barbara, Calif.: Marc-Lard, 1966).

Books on American youth dealing with the more radical politics of the late 1960's which are helpful in understanding the point of view of radicals include Mitchell Goodman,

The Movement Toward a New America: Beginnings of a Long Revolution (New York: Alfred A. Knopf, 1971); Paul Jacobs and Saul Landau, *The New Radicals: A Report with Documents* (New York: Vintage Books, 1966); Peter L. Berger and Richard John Neuhaus, *Movement and Revolution* (New York: Anchor Books, 1970). Perhaps the best of the dozens of books written by young observers of the 1960's is James Simon Kunen's *The Strawberry Statement: Notes of a College Revolutionary* (New York: Random House, 1968).

For a comparative view of young radicals around the world, see Stephen Spender, *The Year of the Young Rebels* (New York: Random House, 1968). For a distinguished anthropologist's view of fundamental change in American culture which bears upon the so-called youth revolution, see Margaret Mead, *Culture and Commitment: A Study of the Generation Gap* (Garden City, N.Y.: Doubleday, 1970); and for an unsympathetic treatment of contemporary youthful unrest within a historical framework, see Oscar Handlin and Mary F. Handlin, *Facing Life: Youth and Family in American History* (Boston: Little, Brown, 1971). Also useful on the history of adolescence is John Demos and Virginia Demos, "Adolescence in Historical Perspective," *Journal of Marriage and Family* (November 1969). The *Fortune* survey frequently cited appeared in the January 1969 issue, devoted to youth.

A number of useful studies exist on adolescence and sex. For a few important examples, see Ira L. Reiss, "Sexual Codes in Teenage Culture," in *Adolescent Development* (Boston: Allyn and Bacon, 1969), edited by Martin Gold and Elizabeth Douvan; Lester A. Kirkendall and Roger W. Libby, "Interpersonal Relationships—Crux of the Sexual Renaissance," *The Journal of Social Issues* (April 1966); Miriam Birdwhistell, "Adolescence and the Pill Culture," *The Family Coordinator* (17), 1968; and Edwin O. Smigel and Rita Seiden, "The Decline and Fall of the Double Standard,"

The Annals of the American Academy of Political and Social Sciences: Sex and the Contemporary Scene (March 1968).

Aging

The literature on the aged in America is growing. For a superb comparative study see Ethel Shanas et al., *Old People in Three Industrial Societies* (New York: Atherton, 1968). For a contrast see Leo W. Simmons, *The Role of the Aged in Primitive Societies* (New Haven, Conn.: Yale University Press, 1945). Also useful to compare is "Social Participation of the Aged in Different Cultures," *Annals of the American Academy of Political and Social Sciences* (279), 1952.

For a look at life from the point of view of older people, see Arnold M. Rose and Warren A. Peterson (eds.), *Older People and Their Social World* (Philadelphia, Pa.: Davis, 1965). Also useful is N. S. Nimkoff, "Changing Family Relationships of Older People in the United States during the Last Fifty Years," *The Gerontologist* (I), 1961; Robert M. Dinkel, "Attitudes of Children Towards Supporting Aged Parents," *American Sociological Review* (9), 1944.

For recent coverage on the picture of the aged in America today, see Esther E. Twente, *Never Too Old* (San Francisco: Jossey-Bass, 1970). Articles which I found helpful include Irving Rosow's "And Then They Were Old," *Transaction* (2), 1965; Mark Messer's "Age Grouping and the Family Status of the Elderly," *Sociology and Social Research* (52), 1968; and "The Couple in Old Age," by Ruth S. Cavan, in *Marriage and the Family in the Modern World* (New York: Crowell, 1969), edited by Ruth S. Cavan. See also R. Brown, "Family Structure and Social Isolation of Older Person," *Journal of Gerontology* (15), 1960. A powerful indictment against American neglect of the aged appears in Jules Henry, *Culture Against Man* (New York: Vintage Books, 1963). There is some evidence that the college-age generation of today is more willing to be helpful in supporting aged parents than their parents were. See Sandra Wake and Michael Sporakowski, "An Inter-generational Comparison of Attitudes Toward Supporting Aged Parents," *Journal of Marriage and the Family* (February 1972).

Chapter III: On Being Female in America

Women in American History

Calhoun, *op. cit.*, is helpful. An older history but still useful is Mary R. Beard's *Woman as a Force in History: A Study in Traditions and Realities* (New York: Macmillan, 1946). A more recent history which includes a chapter on foreign ob-servers is Page Smith's *Daughters of the Promised Land: Wo-men in American History* (Boston: Little, Brown, 1970). An excellent short anthology of writings on women in American history is Anne Fiore Scott (ed.), *The American Woman: What Was She?* (Englewood Cliffs, N.J.: Prentice-Hall, 1971). See also Eugene Leonard, Sophie Drinker, and Miriam Y. Holden, *The American Woman in Colonial and Revolutionary Times, 1565–1800* (Philadelphia: University of Pennsylvania Press, 1961). The literature of feminism has been abundant in recent years. For example, see Judith Hale and Helen Levine, *Rebirth of Feminism* (New York: Quadrangle Books, 1971), and William L. O'Neill, *Everyone Was Brave* (New York: Quadrangle Books, 1969). Two good histories are *The Emancipation of the American Woman* (New York: Harper & Row, 1965), by Andrew Sinclair, and *Century of Struggle* (New York: Atheneum, 1970), by Elea-nor Flexner, which concentrates on the struggle for suffrage. Very useful and balanced anthologies include *Feminism: The*

Essential Historical Writings (New York: Random House, 1972), edited by Miriam Schneir; not nearly as imposing but also useful, *The New Feminism in Twentieth-Century America* (Lexington, Mass.: D. C. Heath, 1971), edited by June Sochen; and *Masculine/Feminine: Readings in Sexual Mythology and the Liberation of Women* (New York: Harper and Row, 1969), edited by Betty Roszak and Theodore Roszak.

The Literature of Revolt

More frankly polemical is *Sisterhood Is Powerful: An Anthology of Writings from the Women's Liberation Movement* (New York: Vintage Books, 1970), edited by Robin Morgan. A socialist orientation in the movement may be found in Evelyn Reed's *Problems of Women's Liberation* (New York: Pathfinder Press, 1971). Five interpretative books which had a profound influence on the development of a new consciousness among women are *The Second Sex* (New York: Bantam Books, 1949), by Simone de Beauvoir; *The Feminine Mystique* (New York: W. W. Norton, 1963), by Betty Friedan; Edith De Rham's *The Love Fraud* (New York: Clarkson N. Potter, 1965); Kate Millet's *Sexual Politics* (Garden City, N.Y.: Doubleday, 1970); and Germaine Greer's *The Female Eunuch* (New York: McGraw-Hill, 1970).

For an excellent history of what women have been complaining about, see Katharine M. Rogers, *Troublesome Helpmate: A History of Misogyny in Literature* (Seattle: University of Washington Press, 1966). But for a very different point of view, excellently developed, which challenges fundamentally some of the assumptions of militant feminism, see Carl Stern, *The Flight from Woman* (New York: Noonday Press, 1965).

Women at Work

Three superb books give a comprehensive view: Robert W. Smuts, *Women and Work in America* (New York: Columbia University Press, 1959); Caroline Bird, *Born Female: The High Cost of Keeping Women Down* (New York: David McKay, 1968); and Cynthia Fuchs Epstein, *Woman's Place: Options and Limits in Professional Careers* (Berkeley: University of California Press, 1971). For a recent empirical study of the housewife, see Helena Znaniecki Lopata, *Occupation Housewife* (New York: Oxford University Press, 1972).

Among the sociologists, Alice Rossi has contributed to my understanding of women, their minds and the world of work. See "Equality between the Sexes: An Immodest Proposal," *Daedalus* (Spring 1964); "Beginning of Ideology," *The Humanist* (Fall 1969). On education, see Thomas Woody, *History of Education in the U.S.* (New York: Octagon Books, 1966); and "Trends in Educational Attainment of Women," U.S. Dept. of Labor, Women's Bureau (October 1969). Also very helpful to me was an unpublished paper "Institutional and Internalized Barriers to Women in Higher Education," by Pamela Roby, Brandeis University. On the law, see Leo Kanowitz, *Women and The Law: The Unfinished Revolution* (Albuquerque: University of New Mexico Press, 1969).

The Sexuality of Women

The two great works are, of course, Alfred C. Kinsey, *Sexual Behavior in the Human Female* (Philadelphia, Pa.: Saunders, 1953); and William H. Masters and Virginia E. Johnson, *Human Sexual Response* (Boston: Little, Brown, 1966).

These two pathfinding empirical studies contrast with the usual material that speculates on female sexuality. But speculations can be helpful in interpreting the data. An important series of articles written from a psychoanalytic point of view appeared in Hendrik M. Ruitenbeck (ed.), *Psychoanalysis and Female Sexuality* (New Haven, Conn.: College and University Press, 1966). A markedly opposed interpretation is Mary Jane Sherfey's *The Nature and Evolution of Female Sexuality* (New York: Random House, 1972). As in other matters, I have learned much from Margaret Mead. See her *Sex and Temperament in Three Primitive Societies* (New York: William Morrow, 1935) and *Male and Female* (New York: William Morrow, 1949). A superb little book by Paul Bohannan was also helpful: *Love, Sex and Being Human* (Garden City, N.Y.: Doubleday, 1969).

Differences Between the Sexes

See Ashley Montagu, *Natural Superiority of Women*, rev. ed. (New York: Macmillan, 1968); Eleanor E. Maccoby, (ed.), *The Development of Sex Differences* (Stanford, Calif.: Stanford University Press, 1966); and Judith M. Bardwick, *Psychology of Women: A Study of Biocultural Conflicts* (New York: Harper & Row, 1971). A word of caution: it is extremely difficult to get significant, reliable findings from the literature on sex differences. The Bardwick book is ambitious in its emphasis on congenital biochemical factors as a basis for differences in the behavior between the sexes, but many of the studies on which it rests have to be repeated—some are not adequate in design. Despite this, the Bardwick book is probably the best ever written on the subject in combining a careful analysis of empirical studies and insightful interpretation of what they mean. For a provocative, open-minded attempt to interpret the extent to which anatomy plays a role in shaping the destiny of the two sexes, see Erik H. Erikson, "Inner and Outer Space: Reflections on Womanhood," *Daedalus* (93), 1964.

Research on the effect of the menstrual period on behavior is consistent. The major book on the subject is Katherine Dalton, *The Pre-Menstrual Syndrome* (Springfield, Ill.: Charles C. Thomas, 1964).

There are other published articles and unpublished papers on the subject of sexual differences which were of considerable help to me. An example of a good article dealing with sex differences in animals which emphasizes the biochemical approach is Seymour Levine, "Sex Differences in the Brain," *Scientific American* (April 1966). An article emphasizing sex differences in mother-infant interactions among monkeys is Gary D. Mitchell's "Attachment Differences in Male and Female Infant Monkeys," *Child Development* (39), 1968. With respect to sex differences in humans, Herbert Barry has done pioneer work. See particularly H. Barry, III, M. K. Bacon, and I. L. Child, "A Cross-Cultural Survey of Some Sex Differences in Socialization," *Journal of Abnormal Social Psychology* (55) 1957; and for a perceptive, wise assessment of the major issues in understanding the differences that differences make, see H. Barry, III, "Cross-Cultural Perspectives on How to Minimize the Adversity Effect of Sex Differentiation," an unpublished paper presented at the Symposium on Behavioral Sciences of the American Psychological Association, Washington, D.C., September 3, 1969. I am also indebted to the commonsense approach of Frank K. Shuttleworth in thinking about differences in male and female sexuality. See his "A Bio-Social and Developmental Theory of Male and Female Sexuality," *Marriage and Family Living* (May 1959). Jerome Kagan's speculation that female precocity in language skills has to do with precocious development of the right hemisphere of the brain was presented in an unpublished paper at Harvard University, November 12, 1970. The material from Beatrice Whiting on consistent sexual differences in six cultures comes from her as yet unpublished book, "Children of Six Cultures."

Much good work is now being done on the socializing or stereotyping of sex roles. Matina Horner has written superbly

on the subject. See "Fail! Bright Women," *Psychology Today*
(November 1969). See also Elizabeth M. Almquist and Shirley S. Angrist, "Role Model Influences on College Women's
Career Aspirations," a paper presented at the session on sex
roles, American Sociological Association, 1970. For the harm
done to females by negative stereotyping, see Paul Rosen-
krantz, Helen Bee, Susan Vogel, Inger Broverman, and Donald Boverman, "Sex-Role Stereotypes and Self-Concepts in
College Students," *Journal of Consulting and Clinical Psychology* (32), 1968.

Brilliant work, much of it unpublished, has been done by
Michael Lewis on the social determinants of sexual differ-
ences. See Susan Goldberg and Michael Lewis, "Play Be-
havior in the Year-Old Infant: Early Sex Differences," *Child
Development* (March 1969); Michael Lewis, "State as an
Infant-Environment Interaction: An Analysis of Mother-In-
fant Behavior as a Function of Sex," *Merrill-Palmer Quar-
terly*, in press; Michael Lewis, "Sex Stereotype Behavior in
Infants: An Analysis of Social-Interpersonal Relationships,"
School Review, in press.

Chapter IV: Flight from Families

Traditional Extended Families

Ariès, *op. cit.*, is helpful, although he talks mainly about
France. On the English, see Peter Laslett, *The World We
Have Lost* (New York: Charles Scribner's Sons, 1965). On
comparisons with the Orient, see David and Vera Mace, *Marriage East and West* (Garden City, N.Y.: Doubleday, 1959);
it contains an excellent bibliography. Useful books on China
are Olga Lang, *Chinese Family and Society* (New Haven,

Conn.: Yale University Press, 1946); and Martin C. Yang, *A Chinese Village* (New York: Columbia University Press, 1954). On the Kikuyu of central Kenya see Jomo Kenyatta, *Facing Mount Kenya* (New York: Vintage Books, 1965).

Fleeing Families

On fleeing families, see Bridges, *op. cit.*, on Thoreau and Emerson, and, of course, Henry David Thoreau, *Walden and Other Writings* (New York: Modern Library, 1937). The literature on evangelical Protestantism and great secular causes is legion. Just two examples are Whitney R. Cross, *The Burned-Over District* (New York: Harper & Row, 1950); and William G. McLaughlin (ed.), *The American Evangelicals, 1800–1900, an Anthology* (New York: Harper & Row, 1968). With respect to psychotherapy, the American psychotherapists mentioned have all done important work. The point is simply that they are all products of the culture in which they live. See William James, *The Principles of Psychology*, Vols. I, II, (New York: Henry Holt, 1890), particularly Chapter 10 in Vol. 1, entitled "The Consciousness of Self," also Gardiner Murphy's *The First Human Nature* (New York: Basic Books, 1958), Part Four, "Self-Directed Change." Murphy emphasizes biosocial factors in the development of personality more than the others. Carl Rogers, a great and perhaps the most influential of American psychotherapists, emphasizes the individual apart from biological, social and historical considerations; see his *Client-Centered Therapy* (Boston: Houghton Mifflin, 1965). Contrast Erik H. Erikson's chapter "Reflections on American Identity" in *Childhood and Society*, rev. ed. (New York: W. W. Norton, 1964). It was Erikson who gave me the idea of combining John Henry and Emerson in the first chapter. Karen Horney in *The Neurotic Personality in Our Time* (New York: W. W. Norton, 1937) emphasized the psychological cost of individualism. So has Erich Fromm in many of his writings. See his famous *The Art of Loving* (New York: Harper & Row, 1956). Andras Angyval, who is less well known, presents a holistic approach to the study of personality which points up the extent to which the individual is dependent on his environment; see his *Foundations for a Science of Personality* (Cambridge, Mass.: Harvard University Press, 1958). The main point, however, is not the difference between the psychotherapists. It is the extraordinary middle-class reliance on psychotherapy in America, as compared with other societies.

The following give a considerable amount of information about basic encounter groups: Jane Howard, *Please Touch: A Guided Tour of the Human Potential Movement* (New York: McGraw-Hill, 1970); John Mann, *Encounter: A Weekend with Intimate Strangers* (New York: Grossman, 1970); Martin Shepard and Marjorie Lee, *Marathon 16* (New York: Putnam, 1970); and Julius Fast, *Body Language* (New York: Evans/Lippincott, 1970). Probably one of the most balanced, expert accounts is Carl Rogers' *Carl Rogers on Encounter Groups* (New York: Harper & Row, 1970).

Communes

The best work on American communes is by Rosabeth Moss Kantor, *Commitment and Community* (Cambridge, Mass.: Harvard University Press, 1972). Her bibliography is exhaustive. See also her "Commitment and Social Organization: A Study of Commitment Mechanisms in Utopian Communities," *American Sociological Review* (August 1968). Among her unpublished work, a paper entitled "Women, Men and the Family in Communal Orders" (1971) was particularly helpful. I also read with interest her "Getting It All Together: Some Group Issues in Communes," a paper delivered at the 1971 meetings of the American Orthopsychiatric Association, Washington, D.C., March 22, 1971.

The best, after Kantor's analysis, of the twentieth-century books on earlier communes is Mark Holloway, *Heavens on Earth, Utopian Communities in America, 1680–1880* (London: Turnstile Press, 1951). Of course, there are individual books or long articles on almost every major communal experiment. See, for example, Edward Deming Andrews, *The People Called Shakers: A Search for a Perfect Society* (New York: Dover, 1963) or Bertha M. Shambaugh, *Amana That Was and Amana That Is* (Iowa City: The State Historical Society of Iowa, 1932). On New Harmony, see George B. Lockwood, *The New Harmony Movement* (New York: D. Appleton, 1905). Of the sizable literature on Oneida, the most recent book is Maren Lockwood Carden, *Oneida: Utopian Community to Modern Corporation* (Baltimore: The Johns Hopkins Press, 1969).

I was introduced years ago to the subject of communes by Charles Nordhoff, *The Communistic Societies of the United States* (New York: Schocken, 1965), first published in 1875. Nordhoff visited Amana, Harmony, Zoar, the Shakers, Oneida and other communes and described in detail what he saw.

There are a great many articles and a few books on contemporary communes. The most comprehensive and descriptive, although not particularly analytical, is *The Alternative: Communal Life in New America* (London: Collier-Macmillan, 1970), by William Wedgepth. A breezy but tough-minded look at communes appears in *The Youth Commune* (New York: Tower Publications, 1970), by Roy Ald. The commune movement has been growing so rapidly that it may be best to keep up with it through *The Modern Utopian,* a magazine about communal experiments and other aspects of the counter-culture. Professor Kantor has also tried to analyze contemporary communes. See "Communes," *Psychology Today* (July 1970).

Bruderhauf and Kibbutzim

On the Bruderhauf see Eberhard Arnold, *Torches Together* (Rifton, N.Y.: Plough Publishing House, 1967), and *The Society of Brothers, Children in Community* (Rifton, N.Y.: Plough Publishing House, 1963).

The literature on the kibbutzim is much more extensive and scholarly. The most recent example, *The Children of the Dream* (New York: Macmillan, 1969), by Bruno Bettelheim, is challenging and controversial but probably wrong, according to many studies to the contrary, in its generalizations on the lack of emotion within the biological family. For a highly informative critical review of the Bettelheim book see Urie Bronfenbrenner, "The Dream of the Kibbutz," *The Saturday Review of Literature* (September 20, 1970). Older but still very useful studies are by Melford E. Spiro, *Kibbutz: Venture in Utopia* (Cambridge, Mass.: Harvard University Press, 1956), and by the same author with the assistance of Audrey G. Spiro, *Children of the Kibbutz: A Study of Child Training and Personality* (Cambridge, Mass.: Harvard University Press, 1958). The emphasis in most writings on the kibbutz is on child-rearing and applies more to the next chapter of this book in which the kibbutzim are also discussed. For an excellent collection of articles, see Peter B. Neubauer (ed.), *Children in Collectives: Child-Rearing Aims and Practices in the Kibbutz* (Springfield, Ill.: Charles C. Thomas, 1965). Two very important articles are Joseph Marcus, "Early Child Development in Kibbutz Group Care," *Early Child Development and Care* (1), 1971; and Joseph Shepher, "Families and Social Structure: The Case of the Kibbutz," *Journal of Marriage and the Family* (August 1969).

Sexual Permissiveness

For anyone who doubts that major changes toward sexual permissiveness have taken place since Kinsey, see Vance

Packard, *The Sexual Wilderness: The Contemporary Up-heaval in Male-Female Relationships* (New York: David Mc-Kay, 1968); Sarah Harris, *The Puritan Jungle: America's Sexual Underground* (New York: Putnam, 1971); Brian Rich-ard Boylan, *Infidelity* (Englewood Cliffs, N.J.: Prentice-Hall, 1971); and Garhard Neubeck (ed.), *Extra-Marital Relations* (Englewood Cliffs, N.J.: Prentice-Hall, 1969), which puts the American picture in cross-cultural perspective.

There is also a growing literature, most of it sensational, on group sex activities. See Paul Rubenstein and Herbert Mar-golis, *The Group Sex Tapes* (New York: David McKay, 1971), and Gilbert D. Bartell, *Group Sex: A Scientist's Eye-witness Report on the American Way of Swinging* (New York: Peter Wyden, 1970). Although loaded with informa-tion, each of these books has its deficiencies. The most sys-tematic, scholarly work on group marriage and multilateral sex is being done by Larry L. and Joan N. Constantine. See their "Group and Multi-lateral Marriage: Definitional Notes, Glossary and Annotated Bibliography," *Family Process* (June 1971); and "Sexual Aspects of Multi-lateral Relations," *The Journal of Sex Research* (August 1971). The annotated bibli-ography had some eighty-one items.

On the Malinowski studies cited, see Ashley Montagu (ed.), *Marriage, Past and Present: A Debate between Robert Briffault and Bronislaw Malinowski* (Boston: Porter Sargent, 1956); and Bronislaw Malinowski, *The Sexual Life of Sav-ages* (New York: Harcourt, Brace & World, 1929), a brilliant anthropological study. Fascinating material on the Kaingang may be found in Stephens, *op. cit.* The Mbuti are described in Colin Turnbull, *Wayward Servants* (New York: Natural History Press, 1965). On hunter-gatherers, see Richard B. Lee and Irven De Vore (eds.), *Man, the Hunter* (Chicago: Al-dine, 1968); and L. Marshall, "The Kung Bushmen of the Kalihari Desert," in J. Gibbs (ed.), *Peoples of Africa* (New York: Holt, Rinehart & Winston, 1965).

On the Unwin book mentioned, see J. D. Unwin, *Sex and Culture* (London: Oxford University Press, 1934). On the Soviet Union, see David and Vera Mace, *The Soviet Family* (Garden City, N.Y.: Doubleday, 1963); and an excellent article by H. Kent Geiger, "The Fate of the Family in Soviet Russia: 1917–1944," in *The Family* (New York: The Free Press, 1968), edited by Norma W. Bell and Ezra F. Vogel. On Samoa, see Margaret Mead's *Coming of Age in Samoa*.

On the subject of momism, the most influential book was Philip Wylie's *A Generation of Vipers* (New York: Rinehart, 1942), which sold about four hundred thousand copies within the first few years of publication. Another rather violent attack on the American mother appears in Ferdinand Lundberg and Marynia A. Farnham, *Modern Women: The Lost Sex* (New York: Grosset & Dunlap, 1947).

For information on breast- and bottle-feeding, see Herman F. Meyer, "Current Trends in Hospital Infant Feeding: A Comparison of Breast and Bottle Feeding Practices in Newborn Nurseries of United States Hospitals, 1946, 1956, 1966," *American Academy of Pediatrics*, 1967. The information on natural childbirth comes from newsletters (1967–1971) of The Boston Association for Childbirth Education.

Chapter V: The Restoration of Father

The Weakening of Male Authority and Men

Two recent volumes attempt to put the decline of father within the context of fundamental social and technological changes in Western society. See Karl Bednarik, *The Male Crisis: The Emasculation of Contemporary Man by the Tech-*

nocratic Society and Super-State He Has Created (New York: Alfred A. Knopf, 1970), a provocative interpretation. See also Alexander Mitscherlich, *Society Without the Father* (New York: Harcourt, Brace & World, 1970), a difficult book to read in translation from the German but with a fascinating chapter on "The Invisible Father."

As for the American father: Geoffrey Gorer, the English anthropologist, begins his study, *The American People* (New York: W. W. Norton, 1948), with an analysis of the American rejection of father. Two other journalistic-sociological accounts also explore the weakened condition of the American male. See Myron Brenton, *The American Male* (New York: Coward-McCann, 1966); and Charles W. Ferguson, *The Male Attitude* (Boston: Little, Brown, 1966).

For a more specific view of how American schools harm male children, see Patricia Cayo Sexton, *The Feminized Male: Classrooms, White Collars and the Decline of Manliness* (New York: Random House, 1971). For a sharp analysis of what the pace of American life does to males, see Selig Greenberg, "Why Women Live Longer than Men," *Harper's Magazine*, October 1957. I am obliged to one of my students, Zoe Levy, for a comprehensive report on comparative statistics of many countries dealing with stuttering, bed-wetting, asthma and reading problems in children. She reported on more than forty such studies. See also, Charles Shaw, *The Psychiatric Disorders of Childhood* (New York: Appleton-Century-Crofts, 1966).

Two unusual small volumes with a religious-counseling orientation deal sensitively and subjectively with feelings of male weakness and frustration. See John H. Ford, *Husband and Father* (St. Neste, Meinrad, Ind.: Abbey Press, 1965); and Urban G. Steinmetz, *The Male Mystique* (Notre Dame; Ind.: Ave Maria Press, 1970).

The neglect of the father as a subject of study has recently been corrected to some extent. For an excellent survey of the literature on the subject, see Leonard Benson, *Fatherhood: A Scoiological Perspective* (New York: Random House, 1971). An excellent chapter on "The American Father" appears in E. E. LeMasters, *Parents in Modern America* (Homewood, Ill.: The Dorsey Press, 1970).

For information and interpretations which relate the ambiguity of male authority to a decline of paternal authority generally, see J. Mogey, "A Century of Declining Paternal Authority," *Marriage and Family Living* (19), 1957; and the sweeping analysis by Louis S. Feuer, who focuses primarily on youth movements but who deals also with the "de-authorization" of parenting in *The Conflict of Generations* (New York: Basic Books, 1969). In a large study (in which only wives were interviewed) dealing with disagreements between husband and wife, 34 percent of the women said they gave in to their husbands, 24 percent said their husbands gave in to them and 40 percent said no one gave in. See Robert O. Blood and Julia and Donald M. Wolf, *Husbands and Wives: The Dynamics of Married Living* (New York: The Free Press, 1960). There is some evidence that egalitarian decision-making provides the most marital satisfaction in middle-class families and that wife-dominant decision-making patterns evoke the least satisfaction for wives and husbands. Following the methodology used by Blood and Wolf, that conclusion was reached in a study of 776 husbands and wives in Los Angeles. See Richard Centers and Bertram Raven, "Conjugal Power Structure: A Re-Examination," *American Sociological Review* (April 1971). There is certainly no evidence to believe that most women want to play the role of super mother to children or husbands.

For an older and more optimistic view on the maintenance of paternal interest, see Ruth J. Tasch, "The Role of the Father in the Family," *Journal of Experimental Education* (June 1952). For data on mothers who think that fathers are tougher in disciplinary matters than mothers, see Daniel R.

Miller and Diese Swanson, *The Changing American Parent* (New York: John Wiley & Sons, 1958). For a contrary and more comprehensive and up-to-date review showing mothers more actively involved in disciplining as well as in other forms of behavior toward children, see "Child Rearing in the United States and England: A Cross-National Comparison," *Journal of Marriage and the Family* (May 1969). On Denmark, see Denise Kandel and Gerald S. Lesser, "Parent-Adolescent Relationships and Adolescent Independence in the United States and Denmark," *Journal of Marriage and the Family* (May 1969). In Israel, the Soviet Union and Denmark, young children are subjected to stronger discipline than in the United States, and by the time they reach adolescence the effect seems to be that they have more self-confidence and self-esteem.

On the significance of consistent paternal authority with respect to the development of self-confidence and self-esteem in children there is a superb survey of the findings in the literature in an article by Diana Baumrind, "Effects of Authoritative Parental Control on Child Behavior," *Child Development* (38), 1966. Baumrind shows how the empirical evidence blasts the assumptions made that permissiveness, or letting children do what they want to do, leads to self-reliance, self-control and self-esteem. The evidence contradicts the assumption that punishment is invariably ineffective or intrinsically harmful. Her bibliography is particularly helpful, but not included in it is a prize-winning study of the relationship between parental and other social influences and self-esteem in children which comes to the same basic conclusion. See Morris Rosenberg, *Society and the Adolescent Self-Image* (Princeton, N.J.: Princeton University Press, 1965), for a study of five thousand American adolescents which concludes that parental indifference is clearly associated with lower self-esteem in the child and is "even more deleterious than punitive parental reactions."

See also an older study, Adelaide M. Johnson and Edmunde C. Burke, "Parental Permissiveness and Fostering in Child Rearing and Their Relationship to Juvenile Delinquency," *Proceedings of the Staff Meetings of the Mayo Clinic* (Rochester, Minn.: November 1955). A very important study (unpublished manuscript, Department of Child Development, Cornell University, 1968) by John C. Condry, Jr., Michael L. Siman, and Urie Bronfenbrenner, "Characteristics of Peer-and-Adult-Oriented Children," makes it clear that those adolescents who are strongly peer-oriented tend to hold negative views of themselves, have less self-confidence—and take a dim view of their own future—than those who are adult-oriented. See also Charles E. Bowerman and John W. Kinch, "Changes in Family and Peer Orientation between the Fourth and Tenth Grades," *Social Forces* (February 1959). For the important distinction between authoritarian and authoritative parenting, see Diana Baumrind, "Authoritarian versus Authoritative Control," *Adolescence* (3), 1968; and also, Lyle E. Larson, *The Structure and Process of Social Influence During Adolescence: An Examination of the Salience Hierarchy* (unpublished doctoral dissertation, University of Oregon, 1969). The study of what it means to be a father and what it means to be a mother to fifth- and sixth-graders was done by one of my students, Leslie Kieter.

The Importance of Mothering

Certain names stand out in the literature on the significance of mothering and each has influenced my thinking: Harlow, Bowlby, Spitz and Brody. It was in his early article "Love in Infant Monkeys," *Scientific American* (June 1959), that Harry F. Harlow sought to bring the study of mother love into the domain of science. Studying rhesus monkeys, Harlow surprisingly found in a series of investigations that newly born monkeys separated from their mothers for a few hours after birth and given the best medical attention and diet eventually became extremely neurotic and incapable of relating to other monkeys. The female monkeys who had been raised in social isolation became what Harlow called "cruel and indifferent mothers," four actually killing their infants and three others being excessively brutal. Later, Harlow investigated the nature of mother love in rhesus monkeys and discovered the importance of close bodily contact; see "The Nature of Love," *American Psychologist* (13), 1958, and "Love in Infant Monkeys," *Scientific American,* June 1959. In addition, see Harry F. and Margaret K. Harlow, "Social Deprivation in Monkeys," *Scientific American* (November 1962).

The extensive work of Renee A. Spitz in the late 1940's and early 1950's probably has been the major source of knowledge about the significance of positive mothering during infancy on the development of a healthy child. From more than a dozen reports of original research, Spitz found that emotional starvation in the first year of life was as destructive to the later development of humans as physical starvation would be. A comprehensive bibliography on Spitz may be found in Sylvia Brody's *Patterns of Mothering: A Study of Maternal Influence During Infancy* (New York: International Universities Press, 1956), a book which constitutes an extraordinary source of information on what is reliably known about all aspects of maternal-infant relationships.

More recently, English psychiatrist John Bowlby has extended the research on the issue of maternal deprivation, and for the most part, reinforced the theory of the primacy of the mother in establishing patterns of health for child and adult development. For recent accounts see John Bowlby, *Attachment,* Vols. I and II, *Attachment and Loss* and *Attachment and Infancy* (London: Hogarth Press, 1969, 1971). Much of Bowlby's work was done in the fifties and has been recently reprinted in the United States. For example, his *Maternal*

Care and Mental Health first appeared in 1951 (World Health Organization, Monograph Series, 2, Geneva, Switzerland), and was reprinted in 1966 (New York: Schocken). For a particularly important article see his "The Nature of the Child's Tie to His Mother," *International Journal of Psychoanalysis* (39), 1958.

For a survey of research on maternal deprivation, see Harold J. Yarrow, "Maternal Deprivation: Toward an Empirical and Conceptual Re-Evaluation," *Psychological Bulletin* (58), 1961. Bowlby's theories about the importance of biological mothering have been criticized by many on the ground that most of the studies of mother-child separation have been based on children in institutions who suffered from overall environmental deprivation, not just maternal deprivation. See Margaret Mead, "Some Theoretical Considerations on the Problem of Mother-Child Separation," *American Journal of Orthopsychiatry* (24), 1954. His theories have also been contradicted by those who believe that despite the significance of mothers in the early months, others—including fathers—can adequately substitute for mothers. See Rochelle T. Waters, "Child Rearing and Women's Liberation" (unpublished paper delivered at Oxford, February 28, 1970). Support for that view comes in an article by Aase Gruda Skard, "Maternal Deprivation: The Research and Its Implications," *Journal of Marriage and the Family* (27), 1965. A number of studies indicate that separation of the mother from the young child during part of the day is not necessarily damaging. For a review of that literature and an excellent bibliography, see Elizabeth Herzog, *Children of Working Mothers* (Washington, D.C.: Children's Bureau, 382, 1960). There is absolutely no evidence that a loving, authoritative replacement for mother—whether father, aunt, or even housekeeper—cannot make up for the love and authority of the biological mother. But the evidence is overwhelmingly against institutional care, no matter how efficient and well organized. Of course, there are many mothers who, for whatever reason, behave as did Harlow's monkey mothers who had been raised in isolation. See Marian A. Morris, "Psychological Miscarriage: An End to Mother Love," *Transaction* (January/February, 1969). There is no question as to the importance of the earliest infant experiences (see Erik H. Erikson on the issue of trust, *Identity and the Life Cycle*, New York: International Universities Press, 1967), but fathers undoubtedly can do more to encourage such trust. In a study of small American children based on interviews with 379 mothers, Robert R. Sears, Eleanor E. Maccoby and Harry Levin do not report father to be much in evidence; see *Patterns of Children Rearing* (Evanston, Ill.: Peterson & Co., 1957). Other studies show remarkably little interaction between father and infant or father and small child.

With respect to mothering in other cultures, I am much indebted to Leigh Minturn and William Lambert, *Mothers of Six Cultures: Antecedents of Child Rearing* (New York: John Wiley & Sons, 1964), which contrasts mothers in Mexico, the Philippines, Okinawa, India and Kenya with those in New England. This volume was the sequel to *Six Cultures: Studies in Child Rearing*, (New York: John Wiley & Sons, 1963), edited by Beatrice Whiting. One gets the clear impression of the primacy of motherhood in the evolution of human families. For a comparative study of the socialization of children by mothers through folk wisdom, see Beatrice Whiting's "Folk Wisdom and Child Rearing," a paper presented at a symposium on "Sources of Knowledge for Child Rearing" at the December 1971 meetings of the American Association for the Advancement of Science. For a comparative look at the socialization process, including the mother's role in it, see a superb anthology edited by John Middleton, *From Child to Adult* (Garden City, N.Y.: The Natural History Press, 1970). On the hunter-gatherer Kung Bushmen and the importance of close mother–infant relationships there is an excellent un-published paper by M. J. Konner, Department of Anthropol-ogy, Harvard University: "Aspects of the Developmental Eth-ology of a Foraging People" (1972). Once again, this is not to say that the functions of mothering cannot be distributed among many individuals. See Susan Goldberg, "Infant Care in Zambia: Measuring Maternal Behavior" (unpublished pa-per, Institute for Social Research, University of Zambia, 1970); and Diane Lusk and Michael Lewis, "Mother-Infant Interaction and Infant Development among the Wolof of Senegal" (Princeton, N.J.: Educational Testing Service, March 1971). The evidence of the preference of Russian mothers for babushkas over child-care facilities comes from Susan Jacoby, "Who Raises Russia's Children?" *The Satur-day Review of Literature* (August 21, 1971). At present, So-viet statistics contend that there are nine million out of thirty million children of preschool age enrolled either in nurseries which take children from two months to three years or in kindergartens which take them from three to seven years, but Jacoby's figures are 10 percent of the Soviet children under age two and 20 percent between three and seven.

To speak of mother–infant relationships one ought to know something of infancy. Two books rich in data are Ivan Brack-bill, *Infancy and Early Childhood* (New York: The Free Press, 1967); and Jerome Kagan, *Change and Continuity in Infancy* (New York: John Wiley & Sons, 1971), probably the best summary of research on infancy by a creative, original investigator in the field.

Society Support Systems

While this book calls for father to take his rightful place as a major support for mother and children, it remains to be seen in the light of the Soviet and Israeli experience how much most men are willing to invest of themselves in fathering.

Much more basic research is needed on the attitude of American males toward fathering.

The social reforms suggested in this chapter are based primarily on the *Report to the President: White House Conference on Children,* 1970 (Washington, D.C.: Superintendent of Documents, U.S. Government Printing Office, 1971). See particularly "Children and Parents" (pp. 241–255). Also, the superb hard-hitting minority report issued by Professor Urie Bronfenbrenner which emphasizes the responsibility of private industry to take action to support American families. See also the section called "Child Care," which was written by a committee chaired by Professor Jerome Kagan. This report constitutes the latest summary of the literature on child care and working mothers.

There is obviously a need for a great deal of research on what Americans want in the way of support systems for families. Community institutions, schools, industry, housing, the media —all can be used to strengthen or weaken families. At present, most public officials and most citizens simply do not think in such terms. Studies on what has been and is being done in the Soviet Union, Israel, Scandinavia or England must be continued and supplemented by considerable research in America itself. In the meantime, recommendations remain largely in the realm of hypothesis.

About the Author

LAWRENCE H. FUCHS is professor of American Civilization and chairman of the Department of American Studies at Brandeis University, where he has been teaching a seminar on the American family since 1965. As chairman of the executive committee of the social studies program of the Educational Development Center, Professor Fuchs has encouraged new approaches to education for parenting and family life.

In 1961 he was appointed by President Kennedy as the first director of the Peace Corps in the Philippines, and temporarily left Brandeis, where he had been serving as dean of faculty. In 1965 he was appointed by the governor of Massachusetts as first chairman of the Commonwealth Service Corps, an organization designed to increase and organize volunteer activity in support of family and other human needs. Professor Fuchs, who has written six books and numerous articles on American life, has also been active in civic and political affairs. He lives in Weston, Massachusetts.